my revision notes

Edexcel GCSE (9–1) History

CRIME AND PUNISHMENT IN BRITAIN

c.1000–PRESENT & WHITECHAPEL c.1870–c.1900

Alec Fisher

HODDER EDUCATION
AN HACHETTE UK COMPANY

For Becky Stanton and the Mill Chase historians of 2017

The Publishers would like to thank the following for permission to reproduce copyright material.

Acknowledgements: mark schemes reproduced by kind permission of Pearson Education Ltd

Photo credits: p41 Jack the Ripper/British Library, London, UK/© British Library Board. All Rights Reserved/Bridgeman Images; **p50** Lordprice Collection/Alamy Stock Photo

Every effort has been made to trace all copyright holders, but if any have been inadvertently overlooked, the Publishers will be pleased to make the necessary arrangements at the first opportunity.

Although every effort has been made to ensure that website addresses are correct at time of going to press, Hodder Education cannot be held responsible for the content of any website mentioned in this book. It is sometimes possible to find a relocated web page by typing in the address of the home page for a website in the URL window of your browser.

Hachette UK's policy is to use papers that are natural, renewable and recyclable products and made from wood grown in well-managed forests and other controlled sources. The logging and manufacturing processes are expected to conform to the environmental regulations of the country of origin.

Orders: please contact Hachette UK Distribution, Hely Hutchinson Centre, Milton Road, Didcot, Oxfordshire, OX11 7HH. Telephone: +44 (0)1235 827827. Email education@hachette.co.uk Lines are open from 9 a.m. to 5 p.m., Monday to Friday. You can also order through our website: www.hoddereducation.co.uk

ISBN: 978 1 5104 0323 9

© 2018 Alec Fisher

First published in 2018 by
Hodder Education
An Hachette UK Company
Carmelite House, 50 Victoria Embankment
London EC4Y 0DZ

www.hoddereducation.co.uk

Impression number   10 9 8 7 6
Year   2022

Cover photo © ermess/Shutterstock
Illustrations by Gray Publishing
Produced and typeset in Bembo by Gray Publishing, Tunbridge Wells, Kent
Printed in India

A catalogue record for this title is available from the British Library.

How to get the most out of this book

This book will help you revise for the Thematic study and historic environment: Crime and punishment in Britain, c1000–present *and* Whitechapel, c1870–c1900: crime, policing and the inner city.

Use the revision planner on pages 2–3 to track your progress, topic by topic. Tick each box when you have:

1 revised and understood each topic
2 completed the activities
3 checked your answers online.

The content in this book is organised into a series of double-page spreads which cover the specification's content. The left-hand page on each spread has key content for each topic, and the right-hand page has one or two activities to help you with exam skills or learn the knowledge you need. Answers to these activities and quick multiple-choice quizzes to test your knowledge of each topic can be found online at www.hoddereducation.co.uk/myrevisionnotes.

At the end of the book is an exam focus section (pages 48–54) which gives you guidance on how to answer each exam question type.

There are a variety of **activities** for you to complete related to the content on the left-hand page. Some are based on **exam-style questions** which aim to consolidate your revision and practise your exam skills. Others are **revision tasks** to make sure that you have understood every topic and to help you record the key information about each topic.

Tick to track your progress as you revise each element of the key content.

Content for each topic is on the left-hand page.

Key terms, **Key individuals** and **Key factors** are highlighted in the section colour the first time they appear, with an explanation nearby in the margin. As you work through this book, highlight other key ideas and add your own notes. Make this *your* book.

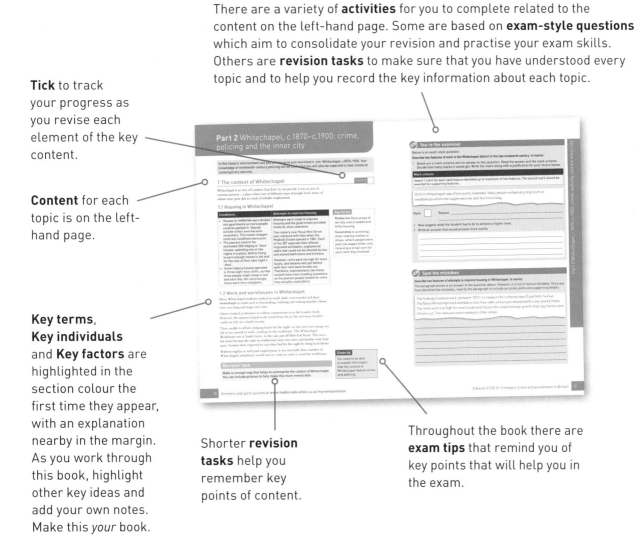

Shorter **revision tasks** help you remember key points of content.

Throughout the book there are **exam tips** that remind you of key points that will help you in the exam.

Contents and revision planner

Part 1 Crime and punishment in Britain, c.1000–present

Crime and punishment in Britain is a development study. It is important that you have a secure chronological understanding of the content – what happened and when. You also need to be able to identify changes and continuities in methods of crime prevention and punishments.

An overview of crime and punishment from c.1000

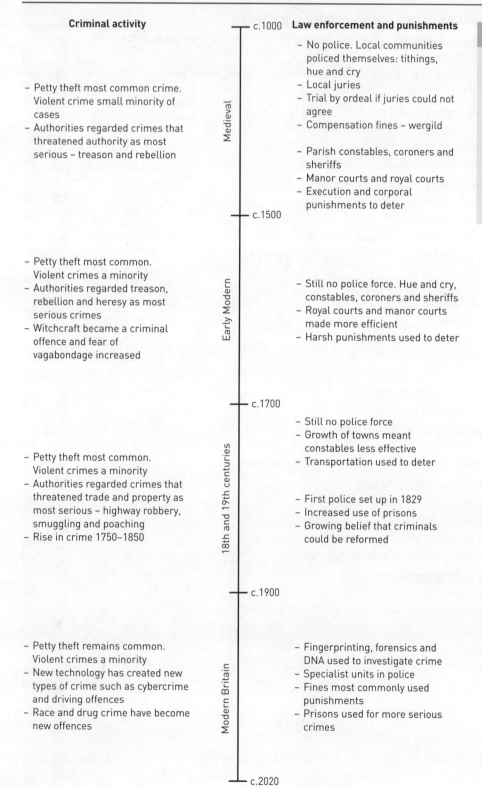

Criminal activity

Law enforcement and punishments

Medieval (c.1000–c.1500)

Criminal activity:
- Petty theft most common crime. Violent crime small minority of cases
- Authorities regarded crimes that threatened authority as most serious – treason and rebellion

Law enforcement and punishments:
- No police. Local communities policed themselves: tithings, hue and cry
- Local juries
- Trial by ordeal if juries could not agree
- Compensation fines – wergild

- Parish constables, coroners and sheriffs
- Manor courts and royal courts
- Execution and corporal punishments to deter

Early Modern (c.1500–c.1700)

Criminal activity:
- Petty theft most common. Violent crimes a minority
- Authorities regarded treason, rebellion and heresy as most serious crimes
- Witchcraft became a criminal offence and fear of vagabondage increased

Law enforcement and punishments:
- Still no police force. Hue and cry, constables, coroners and sheriffs
- Royal courts and manor courts made more efficient
- Harsh punishments used to deter

18th and 19th centuries (c.1700–c.1900)

Criminal activity:
- Petty theft most common. Violent crimes a minority
- Authorities regarded crimes that threatened trade and property as most serious – highway robbery, smuggling and poaching
- Rise in crime 1750–1850

Law enforcement and punishments:
- Still no police force
- Growth of towns meant constables less effective
- Transportation used to deter

- First police set up in 1829
- Increased use of prisons
- Growing belief that criminals could be reformed

Modern Britain (c.1900–c.2020)

Criminal activity:
- Petty theft remains common. Violent crimes a minority
- New technology has created new types of crime such as cybercrime and driving offences
- Race and drug crime have become new offences

Law enforcement and punishments:
- Fingerprinting, forensics and DNA used to investigate crime
- Specialist units in police
- Fines most commonly used punishments
- Prisons used for more serious crimes

Revision task

Create your own crime and punishment timeline by copying the example on this page. Make it bigger. You could use a roll of lining paper. As you work through this book, add key events, individuals and developments to make it more detailed.

The role of factors

Factors are things that influenced crime and punishment in the following ways:

- They helped to cause change: for example, the factor of individuals contributed to improvements in prisons during the nineteenth century through the campaigning of Elizabeth Fry.
- They helped to prevent change: for example, the factor of the government contributed to the continued use of harsh punishment as a deterrent from the late middle ages to the nineteenth century.

The main factors that you could be asked about in your exam are shown in the diagram below, with an explanation of what they mean.

Revision task

Create a table of the factors in each time period that led to a change in crimes, methods of enforcing the law (trials and policing) and punishments.

Individuals: individuals influenced crime and punishment. These were mostly politicians or campaigners who had new ideas about preventing crime and reforming criminals

The institution of the Church: religious ideas sometimes influenced beliefs about trials and how criminals should be punished. Having the wrong religious beliefs was sometimes regarded as a serious crime

Five key factors which encouraged or inhibited change

The institution of the government: the group of people governing the country have had a direct effect on making the laws and deciding on how these were enforced

Attitudes in society: fear of crime helped to encourage the use of harsh punishments for certain offences. The public regarded some illegal acts less seriously. Historians call these social crimes

Science and technology: new discoveries (science) and new inventions (technology) usually encouraged a change. Some were not directly linked to crime and punishment, for example, the printing press, but they still had an impact

Exam tip

Remember that there are other factors that were important in particular periods of history, but not consistently through time. Therefore, you should also consider the effects of *poverty and wealth*, *travel* and *towns* on crime and punishment when planning your answers.

Part 1 Crime and punishment in Britain, c.1000–present

c.1000–c.1500: Crime and punishment in medieval England

Medieval England was ruled by kings who were responsible for making laws and protecting the land from attack. The great majority of people followed the teachings of the Catholic Church and attended services regularly.

1 Anglo-Saxon justice

REVISED

1.1 Anglo-Saxon law enforcement

Anglo-Saxon society was based on close-knit farming communities. The most common crimes were against property, usually petty theft. As there was no police force, local communities played a vital part in policing and trials.

Policing methods	Trials
Tithing: groups of ten men responsible for each other's behaviour. If one broke the law, the others had to bring him to court, or pay a fine.	**Trial by local jury:** a jury of local men who knew the accuser and the accused. If there was no clear evidence, the jury members decided guilt or innocence based on their knowledge of those concerned.
Hue and cry: if an alarm was raised, the entire village had to hunt for the criminal. If someone did not join the hue and cry then the whole village had to pay a heavy fine.	**Trial by ordeal:** if a local jury could not agree, then trial by ordeal was used in the hope that God would decide (see below). All ordeals were taken in or near a church with a priest present.

Key factors

Attitudes in society
Anglo-Saxons lived in small communities and knew their neighbours well. People thought that it was their duty to look out for one another and help to enforce the law.

The Church The Anglo-Saxons were highly religious and believed that God could help to judge crimes. Therefore, they used trial by ordeal.

Types of trial by ordeal:

Trial by cold water	Trial by hot water	Trial by hot iron	Trial by blessed bread
Usually taken by men. The accused was lowered into water on the end of a rope. If the accused sank below the 'pure water' then he was judged innocent. If the accused floated, then he had been 'rejected' by the pure water and was guilty.	Usually taken by men. The accused put his hand into boiling water to pick up an object. The hand was bandaged and unwrapped three days later. A cleanly healing wound meant innocence.	Taken by women. The accused picked up a red-hot weight and walked three paces with it.	Taken by priests. A priest prayed that the accused would choke on bread if they lied. The accused was found guilty if he choked.

1.2 Anglo-Saxon punishments

Anglo-Saxons' punishments were mainly fines but they also used **capital punishment** or **corporal punishment**:

Fines	Capital and corporal punishments
Wergild: compensation paid to the victims of crime or their families. The level of fine was set by the king's laws. Killing a noble was 300 shillings; a freeman was 100 shillings; while the fine for killing a peasant was lower.	**Execution:** the death penalty was used for treason against the king or betraying your lord. This helped to enforce loyalty.
Also used to settle cases of physical injury. Different body parts had different prices, for example, the loss of an eye was worth 50 shillings, whereas a broken arm cost six shillings.	**Mutilation:** reoffenders could lose a hand, an ear or their nose, or even be blinded.

Revision task

Some answers have been provided below and it is your job to come up with suitable matching questions. Try to make each question as detailed as possible so that you are using your knowledge to help you word it.

- hue and cry
- wergild
- tithing
- fine
- trial by ordeal.

Memory map

Create a memory map to show the different ways the Anglo-Saxons dealt with crime and punishment. Add to the map using the information on these two pages. Use key words or phrases. Do not write in full sentences. You could also add some small drawings to help you remember.

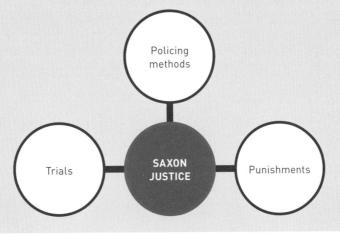

2 The effect of the Norman Conquest on crime and punishment

In the years after the **Battle of Hastings**, King William was faced with controlling 2 million Anglo-Saxons with just 7000 Norman soldiers. Castles appeared all over England and many churches were built or rebuilt in the Norman style. Even the language changed. However, when it came to crime and punishment the Normans also realised the importance of continuity in ensuring control of the population.

2.1 Norman laws

- If a Norman was murdered, all the people of that region had to join together and pay an expensive **Murdrum fine**.
- The majority of Anglo-Saxon laws remained unchanged.
- The much-hated **Forest Laws** were introduced to protect Norman hunting lands. These effectively prevented ordinary people hunting in the forest.
- Medieval chronicles say that England was a safer and more law-abiding place after the Norman Conquest, perhaps suggesting that there was less crime.

2.2 Norman law enforcement

- The Normans kept the local systems of tithings and the hue and cry (see page 6).
- The religious ritual of trial by ordeal continued, but the Normans also introduced trial by combat. The accused fought with the accuser until one was killed or unable to fight on. The loser was then hanged, as God had judged him to be guilty.
- Church courts were established. These were separate courts used for churchmen and tended to be more lenient (see page 12).

2.3 Norman punishments

- The Normans ended wergild (see page 7) – William ordered that fines should no longer be paid to the victim or their family, but to the king's officials.
- The Normans used capital punishment for serious crimes and for reoffenders.

Key terms

Battle of Hastings Key battle in 1066 in which the Normans defeated an Anglo-Saxon army, paving the way for William of Normandy to become King of England.

Forest Laws Trees could no longer be cut down for buildings or fuel. Those living in or near forests were forbidden to own dogs or bows and arrows. Anyone caught hunting deer had their first two fingers chopped off; repeat offenders were blinded.

Murdrum fine The whole community had to pay a heavy fine if any Norman was killed, to deter possible rebellion.

Key factors

The Church The Normans were highly religious and believed that God could help judge crimes. They continued using trial by ordeal and introduced trial by combat, in which victory was thought to be granted by God.

Government King William wanted to be viewed as the rightful heir to the English throne. Therefore, he realised that it was important to keep most of the laws of previous Saxon kings.

Identifying change and continuity

Draw your own large version of the Venn diagram below. Use the information on page 8 to make notes on what the Normans did. Be careful: some things were partly change and partly continuity; put these in the overlap.

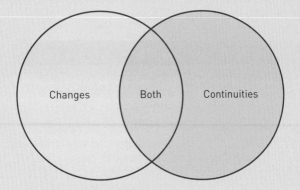

Changes   Both   Continuities

 ## Complete the answer

Below is an exam-style question which asks how far you agree with a specific statement. The paragraph gives an argument for agreeing with the statement but it is not complete.

1   Complete the paragraph to add more supporting knowledge and an explanation linking back to the question.

2   Complete the rest of the answer. Include a further paragraph that considers the other side of the argument and include a conclusion that makes an overall judgement.

'The Norman Conquest saw complete change to law enforcement and punishment in England.' How far do you agree? Explain your answer. (16 marks)

> You may use the following information in your answer:
> ● Forest Laws
> ● Murdrum fine

In some ways, the Norman Conquest did bring changes to law enforcement and punishment because the Forest Laws were introduced to protect Norman hunting land. This stopped people being able to cut trees or hunt red deer in the forest. Even owning a bow and arrow or hunting dogs was made into a crime. Those caught breaking the law were mutilated by having their first two fingers cut off and reoffenders were blinded. This was a big change because it stopped many people from hunting or even collecting wood for fuel. Secondly, the murdrum fine was used if any Norman was killed.

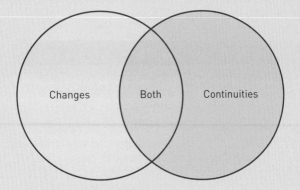

3 Crime and punishment in the later middle ages

During the later middle ages (c.1100–c.1500), medieval kings took an even closer interest in laws, policing, trials and punishments. There was a growing belief that harsh punishments, including execution, were the best way to **deter** criminals.

3.1 Law enforcement in the later middle ages

Policing methods	Trials
As most people still lived in small farming communities, the existing local system of tithings and the hue and cry continued.	Manor courts were local courts used to deal with minor crimes.
Village **constables** were appointed annually to look out for crime and lead the hue and cry when necessary. These unpaid volunteers were well-respected members of the community.	Royal judges travelled around the country hearing more serious cases. The juries for manor and royal courts were from the local area.
Coroners were royal officials. All unnatural deaths had to be reported to the coroner for further investigation.	Trial by ordeal was abolished in 1215.
Each county had a sheriff who, if the hue and cry had failed, was responsible for assembling a **posse** to hunt down criminals.	

3.2 Punishments in the later middle ages

Fines	Public humiliations	Capital punishment
Most minor crimes were punished with fines paid to the king's officials.	**Stocks** and **pillories** were used to punish certain crimes including selling weak beer or underweight bread. Whipping was often used in public along with the stocks and pillories. Such punishments were intended to deter.	The use of execution increased during this period. Hanging was seen as a necessary public deterrent to reduce crime.

There were several ways for convicted criminals to avoid the death penalty. Men could opt to fight in the army at times of war. Pregnancy protected some women from execution. However, it was the Church that played the biggest role in helping people to avoid execution. Those who could read might claim benefit of the **clergy** (see page 12) and demand to be tried in a Church court. Church courts were more lenient than the royal court and never sentenced people to death. Moreover, if a criminal could reach a church and claim sanctuary (see page 12) not even the sheriff could remove him or her as long as the accused agreed to leave the country.

Key terms

Clergy Archbishops, bishops, priests, monks and other churchmen.

Constables Men from every village or town appointed to uphold law and order. They did this in their own time and received no payment.

Deter To use harsh punishments to scare or warn people not to commit crimes.

Pillory A wooden frame with holes in it that locked in the head and hands of the offender.

Posse A group of men aged fifteen and over called on by the sheriff to track down a criminal.

Stocks A wooden frame with holes in it that locked in the feet of the offender.

Revision task

Using flashcards is an effective way of helping you to remember key details about crime and punishment. Making the flashcards is itself an act of revision and using the flashcards to test yourself will help to reinforce your learning.

1 Make a flashcard for each of the policing methods, trials and punishments that were used in the later middle ages. Put the key term on one side and a brief description on the other. Keep the description as short as possible.

2 Ask a friend or family member to help test your knowledge.

Organising knowledge

It is important to get the big picture of change and continuity across the whole of the medieval period c.1000–c.1500. Complete the table below to show how far crime and punishment developed between the Saxon and Norman era and the later middle ages.

	Situation in 1100	Changes made by kings	Continuities
Policing	• No police force. • Tithings were organised to bring accused to court. • Hue and cry used to catch criminals.		
Trials	• Royal courts for serious cases; manor courts for others. • Local juries decided guilt or innocence. • If jury could not decide then ordeal was used – God was judge. • More lenient Church courts used for clergy		
Punishments	• The Normans ended wergild and fines were paid to the king. • Serious crimes and reoffenders were punished by death.		

4 Case study: Did the Church help or hinder justice in the early thirteenth century?

The Church and religious beliefs played an important part in medieval law and order. Even after trial by ordeal (see page 6) was abolished in 1215, the Church continued to have powerful influence on justice.

4.1 Sanctuary

If someone on the run from the law could reach a church, he or she could claim sanctuary. Once criminals reached sanctuary, they were under the protection of the Church. Even the county sheriff could not remove them.

The criminals had 40 days either to face trial or to leave the country. Those choosing to leave walked, barefoot and carrying a wooden cross, to the nearest port and boarded the first ship overseas.

4.2 Church courts

The Church claimed the right to try any churchman accused of a crime in its own courts. Unlike ordinary courts, Church courts never sentenced people to death, no matter how serious the crime committed.

Church courts also dealt with a range of moral offences including failure to attend church, swearing, drunkenness, adultery and playing football on a Sunday. In this way, it helped to control the lives of ordinary people.

4.3 Benefit of the clergy

Benefit of the clergy was the claim by an accused person to be tried in the more lenient Church courts. In theory, this was intended only for priests. In practice, anyone loosely connected with the Church, such as church doorkeepers or gravediggers, used it to escape tougher punishments.

The Church used a test requiring the accused to read a verse from the Bible. This helped to weed out non-churchmen who, unlike priests, were usually unable to read. However, some criminals learned the words by heart. This was known as the 'neck verse' because it could literally save your neck from the hangman's noose.

4.4 Trial by ordeal

Up until 1215, trial by ordeal provided an outcome if a local jury could not reach a verdict. However, this was based more on luck than on real guilt or innocence. Therefore, guilty criminals could escape punishment and the innocent could be punished. The idea behind trial by combat was similar. If the accused was innocent, then God would grant him victory. If he was guilty then God ensured his defeat. In reality, the outcome of trial by combat depended more on strength.

Exam tip

It is not enough to simply list or describe the features of the Church. The examiner wants you to be able to explain *how* these helped or hindered justice.

Making a judgement

Draw your own copy of the pendulum below to show how much of a help or hindrance to medieval justice each type of Church involvement was. Use the information on page 12 to mark on sanctuary, Church courts, benefit of the clergy and trial by ordeal. Add a couple of sentences explaining in what ways it helped or hindered justice.

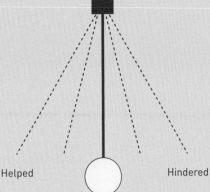

Helped   Hindered

 Eliminate irrelevance

Below is an exam-style question:

Explain why the Church sometimes hindered justice in the early thirteenth century. (12 marks)

> You may use the following information in your answer:
> - Trial by ordeal
> - Sanctuary

1. Below is a paragraph which is part of an answer to the above question. Some parts of the answer are not relevant to the question being asked. Draw a line through any irrelevant information that does not directly help to answer the question.
2. Add one more reason of your own that helps to answer the question.

During the medieval period, the Church had great power and authority. England was a very religious society and the overwhelming majority of people, including monarchs, took the teachings of the Catholic Church very seriously indeed. One way the Church and religious ideas hindered justice was through the use of trial by ordeal. This was used if a local jury was unable to reach a verdict. There were four different types of trial by ordeal. These were trial by hot iron, trial by hot water, trial by cold water and trial by consecrated bread. Trial by cold water was usually taken by men. The accused was tied with a knot above the waist and lowered into the water on the end of a rope. If the accused sank below God's 'pure water' then he was judged innocent. If the accused floated, then he had been 'rejected' by the pure water and was guilty. The idea behind trial by ordeal was that God would help to judge guilt or innocence through sending a sign such as the accused sinking in trial by cold water. However, this sign was based more on luck than on actual guilt or innocence and so the guilty might go free while the innocent were punished.

Secondly, if a criminal on the run reached a church they could claim sanctuary. This put them under the protection of the Church. Even the county sheriff could not remove them. The criminal then had 40 days to face trial or leave England. Those who chose to leave had to walk, barefoot and carrying a wooden cross, to the nearest port to board the first ship overseas. This meant even criminals who had committed serious crimes could escape justice altogether.

c.1500–c.1700: Crime and punishment in early modern England

This was a time of increasing wealth for some and increasing poverty for others. Rich landowners had a growing influence on laws and punishments and dramatic religious changes also affected crime and punishment.

1 Nature and changing definitions of criminal activity (1)

REVISED

1.1 Heresy and treason

For hundreds of years, everyone in England belonged to the Catholic Church led by the Pope. However, during the **Reformation**, new **Protestant** ideas were challenging that authority. Religious changes made by the Tudors caused unrest and confusion as the official religion kept changing. Those with the wrong beliefs at the wrong time could find themselves accused of **heresy** or **treason**.

Henry VIII (r. 1509–47).	In 1534, after the Pope refused to approve his divorce, Henry VIII split with the Catholic Church and made himself Head of the Church in England.	Those refusing to accept the split with the Catholic Church were executed. Henry used Protestant ideas to justify his divorce, but in his heart, was still a Catholic.
Edward VI (r. 1547–53).	Edward further widened the split with the Catholic Church.	Edward made laws requiring the people to worship in a much more Protestant way.
Mary (r. 1553–58).	Mary was determined to make England a Catholic country once more.	Mary ordered the burning of nearly 300 Protestants for heresy. They were given the choice to 'turn or burn' but refused to change their beliefs.
Elizabeth (r. 1558–1603).	Elizabeth was a Protestant. At first, some compromises were made towards the Catholics but England remained firmly Protestant.	Catholics were fined for not attending church and could be locked up for taking part in Catholic services. However, these laws were not strictly enforced. After various plots to kill her, and replace her with a Catholic monarch, around 250 Catholics were executed for treason.

Key terms

Hanging, drawing and quartering Offenders were hanged by the neck, gutted, beheaded and cut into four. Carried out in public to deter traitors.

Heresy The crime of holding religious beliefs different from those of the monarch or Church. The punishment was public burning at the stake.

Protestant The name given to those whose ideas conflicted with the Catholic Church.

Reformation A period of violent religious change, especially in northern Europe, when Protestant Christians rejected the Roman Catholic Church.

Treason Disobedience or disloyalty to the monarch. The punishment was hanging, drawing and quartering.

Revision task

Make a mind map to show the religious changes made under Henry VIII, Edward VI, Mary, Elizabeth and James.

1.2 Case study: The Gunpowder Plot of 1605

When James I (r. 1603–25) became king, Catholics hoped to worship freely. However, the laws against Catholics were tightened and more harshly enforced. Most Catholics had little choice but to accept the changes. However, a few determined plotters chose to act.

Aims	The plot	What happened
Robert Catesby hatched a plan to blow up Parliament, kill King James and put a Catholic on the throne.	Guy Fawkes placed 36 barrels of gunpowder beneath the Houses of Parliament, more than enough to destroy the building and everyone in it.	An anonymous letter warned Lord Monteagle (a Catholic) not to attend the opening of Parliament. Monteagle informed Robert Cecil – the king's chief minister.
		Soldiers searched Parliament and arrested Fawkes. He was tortured and identified the other plotters. When soldiers caught up with them, Catesby and a few of the other plotters were killed in the fighting. The survivors returned to London for trial. They were sentenced to be **hanged, drawn and quartered**.

 Spot the mistakes

Explain why heresy was so harshly punished c.1500–c.1700. (12 marks)

The paragraph below is part of the answer to the question above. However, it is full of factual mistakes. Once you have identified the mistakes, rewrite the paragraph.

Heretics were punished harshly in the period c.1500–c.1700 because there was religious unrest and confusion when Protestant ideas challenged the Catholic Church. Firstly, the official religion in England kept changing under the Tudors. Queen Mary broke with the Catholic Church in order to get a divorce and this split further widened under Elizabeth. However, Edward attempted to turn the clock back and restore the Catholic faith. People found it difficult to keep up with these changes and were sometimes reluctant to change their religious beliefs. As a result, Edward took harsh measures to persuade them by burning Catholic heretics at the stake. Secondly, these harsh punishments were carried out in private in order to deter others from sharing such beliefs.

2 Nature and changing definitions of criminal activity (2)

2.1 Growing fears of 'vagabondage'

By the sixteenth century, a rising population and fewer jobs meant that more people were moving around looking for work. Therefore, the authorities grew very concerned about vagabondage and as attitudes hardened, so too did punishments. Between 1531 and 1598 a series of Vagrancy Acts were introduced to deter others from committing the same offence. Vagabonds were whipped, mutilated and, in certain years, executed.

The government, landowners and better-off members of society worried about **vagabondage** for the following reasons:

- The Bible taught that 'the Devil makes work for idle hands'. Those not working might be tempted to commit sins and turn to crime.

- There was suspicion that vagabonds were professional criminals who chose not to work and were therefore undeserving of any help or charity.

- There was fear that vagabonds formed organised criminal gangs and even spoke their own secret language to plan their crimes.

- The better-off members of the community already paid **poor rates** to support the poor in their own **parish**. They did not want to pay extra to support poor people from other areas.

- After printing was invented in the fifteenth century, more books, broadsheets and **pamphlets** started to appear. A favourite topic was crime, particularly witchcraft (see page 18) and vagabondage. These greatly influenced people's attitudes and further increased fear of vagabonds, who were portrayed as professional criminals.

2.2 The reality of vagabondage

A big problem facing those looking for work in this period was the increasing population. Simply put, there were more people with not enough work to go around. The result was rising unemployment.

Some vagabonds were demobilised soldiers no longer needed in the army after wars ended. However, the majority of vagabonds were ordinary unemployed people looking for work wherever they could find it.

Bad harvests and falling wages also led to a growth in the number of vagabonds. As poverty increased, people travelled elsewhere looking to improve their prospects.

Key terms

Pamphlets Cheap and popular printed news stories. They often contained exaggerated tales of crime.

Parish A local area centred on a church.

Poor rates Tax paid by the wealthier members of a parish to provide relief for the poor.

Vagabondage The then criminalised act of homeless people begging. Also known as vagrancy.

Exam tip

It is not enough to simply describe attitudes towards vagabondage. The examiner wants you to explain how these influenced the government's response to the crime.

Analysing factors

You need to understand the role that factors had on the growth of vagabondage in the sixteenth century and the response of the authorities. Complete the chart below. For each factor, use the information on page 16 to explain how it had an influence on the crime of vagabondage.

Factor	Influence on vagabondage
The Church.	
Government.	
Attitudes in society.	
Science and technology.	

Add any reasons of your own that you think also had an influence.

Identify the view

Read the exam-style question below and identify the view that is offered about the reasons for vagabondage.

'Vagabondage was regarded as a serious threat in the sixteenth century as the result of religious ideas.' How far do you agree? Explain your answer. (16 marks)

1 What is the view offered by the statement about vagabondage?

_____

_____

2 How far do you agree? Use your knowledge to agree and disagree with the statement given in the question. To plan your answer, complete the following table:

Knowledge which agrees with the statement	
Knowledge which disagrees with the statement	

3 Now write paragraphs that agree and disagree with the statement.

The statement is partially correct …

The statement is partially incorrect …

3 Case study: Matthew Hopkins and witchcraft

Between 1645 and 1647, there were many cases of witchcraft in East Anglia. At the centre of this was Matthew Hopkins, a man known as the Witchfinder General due to his 'ability' to spot witches. However, there were several other important reasons why witchcraft became regarded as a serious crime in the early modern period.

3.1 Reasons for the rise in accusations of witchcraft

Village tensions

In times of poverty, poorer people asked their neighbours for help more often. Some villagers felt threatened by such demands. Most people believed that harmful magic could injure or even kill others. Therefore, poor vulnerable women, usually elderly, were sometimes blamed if illness or accident struck.

Changes to the law

During the middle ages, witchcraft was dealt with by more lenient Church courts (see page 12). However, under Henry VIII, Elizabeth and James I the laws were tightened. Witchcraft became a serious criminal offence, punishable by death.

Religious upheavals

Protestants (see page 14) preached that the Devil was tempting good Christians away from God. Superstitious talk of the Devil made people fearful and more likely to look to believe in harmful magic.

The Civil War 1642–49

The **Civil War** sometimes led to a breakdown in the rule of law. The fighting meant that royal judges were less able to travel and so superstitious locals often took cases into their own hands.

Pamphlets

Cheap, printed pamphlets often dealt with dramatic cases of witchcraft. These were widely read and kept the idea of harmful magic firmly in the public imagination.

3.2 The role of Matthew Hopkins 1645–47

- Hopkins and his assistant searched East Anglia for witches and collected evidence against 36 people, mostly elderly women.

- Hopkins got confessions by keeping suspects standing, on the move and awake for days. If a mouse, fly or spider found its way into the room, Hopkins claimed that it was a '**familiar**'. Any scar, boil or spot was regarded as a 'Devil's mark' from which familiars sucked the witch's blood.

- Towns and villages across the region summoned Hopkins to rid them of their witches. Hopkins charged for his services, demanding a fee plus expenses for his time.

3.3 Trial and punishment for witchcraft

The accusers would present their charge and bring witnesses to court to support it. If the accused failed to defend themselves then they were tested further.

The 'swim test' was similar to medieval trial by cold water (see page 6). Accused people had their hands bound and a rope tied around their waists before being lowered into the water. If they floated, the accused would be examined for the 'Devil's marks' as a final proof of witchcraft. Those found guilty were hanged.

Key terms
Civil War The war between the Royalist forces of King Charles I and the armies of Parliament.
Familiar A creature created by the Devil to do the witch's bidding. It supposedly granted the witch magical powers and in return fed on her blood.

Analysing factors

Support each of the statements below with relevant detailed knowledge:

- Witchcraft accusations increased as a result of government action.
- Witchcraft accusations increased as a result of attitudes in society.
- Fear of witchcraft increased as a result of religious beliefs.

 Making comparisons

Look at the exam-style question below and the two answers. Which answer is better for comparing the key features? Why?

Explain one way trials in medieval England were similar to trials in the seventeenth century. (4 marks)

Trials in medieval England and the seventeenth century were similar because they both sometimes used a type of ordeal involving cold water to decide guilt or innocence.

Both the middle ages and the seventeenth century sometimes used a form of trial by cold water. In the middle ages the accused was tied with a knot above his or her waist and lowered into the water on the end of a rope. During the seventeenth century, the 'swimming' test was used in cases of witchcraft to decide whether the accused was guilty. It was believed the innocent would sink and the guilty would float. If he or she floated, the accused would be examined for the 'Devil's marks' as a final proof of witchcraft.

4 The nature of law enforcement and punishment (1)

Between 1500 and 1700, various changes were made to improve law enforcement. However, there were also continuities and responsibility remained with the local community to catch criminals and bring them to justice.

4.1 Policing

Continuities since the late middle ages	Changes
The hue and cry was still used. If the alarm was raised, citizens had to turn out and look for the criminal. This was led by the constable. Citizens (ordinary people) were still expected to deal with crime themselves. If someone was robbed it was his or her responsibility to track down the criminals and deliver them to the constable. Constables continued to have an unpaid and part-time role. They did not go out on patrol and spent most time dealing with everyday matters such as begging or drunkenness. Constables had the power to inflict some punishments, such as whipping vagabonds. Coroners still investigated unnatural deaths.	Watchmen were employed in larger towns to patrol the streets day and night. They were expected to arrest drunks and vagabonds. Watchmen were allowed to peer into windows to look out for crimes. They were poorly paid and often of little use. Rewards were offered for the arrest of particular criminals accused of serious crimes. Rewards could be very high indeed – equal to a year's income for a middle-class family.

Key terms

Habeas Corpus Literally means 'you have the body'. It is an order for an accused person to be brought before a judge or court to establish on what charges they are being held. This prevents unlawful imprisonment.

Justices of the Peace (JPs) Local officials appointed to keep the peace and judge cases. They were usually well-off landowners and people of local importance.

Watchmen Men who patrolled the streets trying to prevent crime.

4.2 Trials

Continuities since the late middle ages	Changes
There were a variety of courts in use but all still relied on a local jury. Manor courts dealt with local, minor crimes such as selling underweight bread and drunkenness. Royal judges visited each county twice a year to deal with the most serious offences. These were known as County Assizes.	Justices of the Peace (JPs) became an important part of local law enforcement. JPs judged manor court cases. They could fine people, send them to the stocks or the pillory, and order them to be whipped. They were assisted by the constable. Quarter Sessions were held four times a year. JPs from across the county would come together to judge more serious cases. They even had the power to sentence someone to death. Those accused of committing serious crimes could no longer claim benefit of the clergy (see page 12). The *Habeas Corpus* Act of 1679 meant that everyone arrested had to appear in court or be released. People no longer feared being seized and locked up without trial.

Revision task

Some answers have been provided below and it is your job to come up with suitable matching questions. Try to make each question as detailed as possible so that you are using your knowledge to help you word it.

- Watchmen
- Justice of the Peace
- *Habeas Corpus*
- Quarter Sessions
- County Assizes

- Manor court
- Royal court
- Unpaid and part-time
- Unnatural deaths
- Equal to a year's income.

Change and continuity spectrum

Make your own copy of the spectrum below. Mark on where you think policing methods and trials go. Add annotations to explain your view and support with specific factual details.

Mainly continuity   Mainly change

Memory map

Create a memory map to show the different ways the law was enforced c.1500–c.1700. Add to the map using the information on page 20. Use key words or phrases. You could use one colour for changes and another for continuities. Do not write in full sentences. You could also add some small drawings to help you remember.

Policing — **LAW ENFORCEMENT c.1500–c.1700** — Trials

5 The nature of law enforcement and punishment (2)

In 1688, changes to the law greatly increased the number of crimes carrying the death penalty. This increase continued throughout the eighteenth and early nineteenth centuries. Even minor crimes were punishable by death – it is no wonder that these laws were known as the 'Bloody Code'.

5.1 Reasons why the Bloody Code was introduced

The Bloody Code was introduced at a time when the amount of recorded crime appears to have been falling. However, people at the time did not know this. They believed that rising crime was a continuing problem:

Increased fears of crime	The growth of towns
Cheaply available printed pamphlets frequently carried stories on crime. This helped create the impression that crime was rising rapidly.	Since the middle ages, towns had grown in number and in population. This made the hue and cry and parish constables less effective as people no longer knew their neighbours.
Executions were in public, which had the effect of publicising crime even further. Moreover, speeches made by those about to hang were often published for the public to read.	The streets in towns were more crowded so it was easier for criminals to commit crimes and escape detection.
Traditional views of punishment	**Landowners' attitudes**
Since the middle ages, harsh punishments had been used to deter criminals. People still believed that this was the only effective way to reduce crime.	The government, who passed the laws that made up the Bloody Code, was made up of wealthy landowners. They feared the large numbers of poor people and saw them as a threat to their property and privileges.
	Landowners believed that only very harsh punishments would keep the poor in their place.

5.2 Other punishments

You need to understand the other types of punishment in use between 1500 and 1700. These ranged from corporal punishment (intended to inflict pain) to public humiliation, fines and even the removal from society of the criminal altogether.

- Stocks and pillories (see page 10).
- Whipping – usually took place in public on market day.
- Fines were the most common punishment and were used for minor offences such as swearing, gambling, drunkenness and failure to attend church.
- Houses of correction were built. Inmates were whipped and made to do hard labour. The authorities believed that some offenders might mend their ways if taught the value of hard work.
- Prisons were only used for those awaiting trial and for people in debt. Ducking stools were used to punish women who argued with their husbands or swore in public.
- From the 1660s, criminals began to be sent thousands of miles away to the American colonies. This was called 'transportation'. Once in America, some prisoners suffered conditions close to slavery.

Change and continuity spectrum

Go back to the spectrum you annotated on page 21. Mark on where punishments should go and annotate it with a simple explanation and specific factual detail.

What do you notice? Was there more change to policing, trials or punishment in the period c.1500–c.1700?

 ## You're the examiner

Below is an exam-style question.

Explain why punishments became harsher with the introduction of the Bloody Code in the period c.1500–c.1700. (12 marks)

You may use the following information in your answer:
- Attitudes in society
- The growth of towns

Below are a mark scheme and a paragraph which is part of the answer to the question. Read the paragraph and the mark scheme. Decide which level you would award the paragraph. Write the level below, along with reasons for your choice.

Remember that for the higher levels you must:
- explain *three* reasons
- focus directly on the question
- support reasons with precise details.

Mark scheme	
Level	
1	A simple or generalised answer is given, lacking development and organisation.
2	An explanation is given, showing limited analysis and with only an implicit link to the question.
3	An explanation is given, showing some analysis, which is mainly directed at the focus of the question.
4	An analytical explanation is given which is directed consistently at the focus of the question.

The Bloody Code was the big increase in the number of crimes that carried the death penalty as punishment. This was partly the result of the growth in towns since the late middle ages. There were simply too many people in such towns for the hue and cry or constables to deal with. These policing methods were originally used in small villages where everyone knew each other and so were much less effective in towns.

Level ☐   Reason _____

_____

1   Now suggest what the student has to do to achieve a higher level.

_____

_____

2   Now try and rewrite this answer at a higher level.

The **Industrial Revolution** changed society, therefore influencing crime and punishment. Definitions of crime and ideas about policing and punishments began to change.

1 Nature and changing definitions of criminal activity (1) REVISED

- Fear of heresy and vagabondage had declined. Laws against witchcraft were scrapped in 1736 as belief in magic declined. The government was more worried about crimes that disrupted trade and the economy or threatened property.

1.1 Highway robbery

Highway robbers were greatly feared by travellers and the government saw them as a major disruption to trade, especially on the roads around London. **Highway robbery** grew as certain changes created opportunities for the robbers. However, highway robbery declined just as quickly as it grew.

Reasons for growth of highway robbery	Reasons for decline in highway robbery
More people were travelling in their own coaches.	The number of banks grew. Therefore, fewer travellers carried large amounts of money.
Handguns were easier for robbers to obtain and became quicker to load and fire.	Stagecoaches were introduced with regular staging posts where tired horses were changed and travellers rested in safety for the night.
Horses became cheaper to buy.	Road surfaces improved and coaches became more frequent as speeds increased.
There were lonely areas outside towns where coaches could be ambushed.	Lonely areas of land around London and other towns were built on as the population expanded.
Highwaymen hid and sold their stolen loot in inns and taverns.	Mounted patrols were set up around London (see the Fielding brothers, page 28) and rewards encouraged informers to identify robbers.
There was no police force and local constables did not track criminals across counties.	Local governments closed down inns and taverns where highwaymen were known to hide or sell their loot.
After wars ended, demobilised soldiers struggled to find honest ways to make a living.	

Key terms

Highway robbery Stopping a coach and robbing the passengers.

Industrial Revolution Technological improvements leading to more factories and towns.

Poaching The illegal hunting of animals.

Smuggling Bringing illegal goods into the country or not paying duty (import tax) on legal goods.

1.2 Smuggling and poaching

Smugglers brought goods into the country without paying any duties (import tax) on them. They supplied a network of traders who sold tea, brandy and other smuggled goods to the public.

Duties were the main source of government income. Therefore, the authorities took **smuggling** very seriously and made it punishable by death. However, there were too few customs officers to enforce the law and the government could not afford to increase their numbers.

Poaching laws meant that only landowners with land worth more than £100 a year (roughly ten years of a labourer's wage) could hunt. The 1723 Waltham Black Act made hunting deer, hare or rabbits a capital crime.

Historians have described poaching and smuggling as social crimes: people knew they were crimes but regarded the law as unfair.

	Government view	Public attitudes
Smuggling	Smuggling was disruptive to trade and a drain on tax revenue. An estimated 3 million pounds weight (1.4 tonnes) of tea was smuggled into Britain each year, with no tax paid. Smuggling gangs could be as large as 50–100 men and were well armed. Gangs fought with **customs men** and even seized back goods that had been confiscated. The government used the army against the larger gangs.	The public disliked expensive duties. Smuggling made luxury goods affordable. Even respectable government ministers were known to have paid for smuggled wine. People usually turned a blind eye to smuggling. In coastal areas, it provided the unemployed and low paid with the chance to make good money. Locals who helped the smugglers carry goods from ship to shore could earn twice the average labourer's daily wage. Fear of gangs deterred the public from giving evidence in court as witnesses were sometimes murdered.
Poaching	Poachers were regarded as a threat to wealthy landowners' property.	People believed that the law favoured rich landowners and that punishments for poaching were too harsh. People in the countryside saw poaching as their age-old right. **Gamekeepers** were generally hated. Villagers frequently lied in court to protect poachers from conviction. Poaching provided food for the pot and supplemented low wages.

✎ Analysing factors

Which of the factors below influenced highway robbery, poaching and smuggling? Think about the growth of these crimes and the reactions of the public and the authorities. Fill in the table, using these two pages to help you.

	Highway robbery	Poaching	Smuggling
The role of individuals.			
The Church and religious ideas.			
The role of government.			
Attitudes in society.			
Science and technology.			
Poverty and wealth.			
Travel.			
Towns.			

Revision task

It is important to understand how definitions of crime changed over time. Make a concept map showing the changing definitions of crime in the eighteenth and nineteenth centuries.

Key terms

Customs men Officials who tried to prevent smuggling.

Gamekeeper Person paid to to protect game from poachers.

2 Nature and changing definitions of criminal activity (2)

REVISED

2.1 The Tolpuddle Martyrs

After the **French Revolution** in 1789, the government was terrified of the same thing happening in Britain. Fearful landowners and politicians viewed every protest as a potential riot or uprising.

The government was particularly concerned about the Grand National Consolidated Trades Union (GNCTU), which aimed to bring workers together to fight for better pay and conditions. It was not illegal to belong to a **trade union**, but employers and the government disliked the idea of working people cooperating. Employers believed that unions threatened their profits and harmed their interests. The story of the Tolpuddle **Martyrs** reveals much about these attitudes and how the government used the law to protect the interests of landowners and employers.

Who were they?

- Six farm labourers in the Dorset village of Tolpuddle led by George Loveless.
- Their wages had been cut several times and they struggled to support their families.

What did they do?

- In 1833, after a further cut to their wages, the men set up a union, the Friendly Society of Agricultural Labourers.
- Each man was blindfolded and swore an oath of secrecy and support for the union.

How did the authorities respond?

- The authorities arrested the six men using a law originally meant for the navy. It prevented sailors taking secret oaths that could lead to mutiny.
- The government used the law to include all secret oaths and the men were sentenced to seven years' transportation to Australia (see page 30). This was intended to deter others from involvement in trade unions.
- The trade union movement was badly hit and the GNCTU was broken up.

What was the public reaction?

- There was widespread outcry. The men were regarded as martyrs for union rights. A campaign was organised and a petition demanding their return was signed by 250,000 people.
- In March 1836, the government granted all six men a pardon. However, it was another two years before all the men were able to return home.
- Workers continued to feel wary about joining trade unions and it was twenty years before the movement began to recover.

Key terms

French Revolution The French monarchy was overthrown and thousands were killed.

Martyr Someone who makes a sacrifice and suffers for his or her beliefs.

Trade union An organisation of workers set up to defend their interests and improve their working conditions.

Key factors

Attitudes in society Large numbers of people felt that the Tolpuddle Martyrs were punished unfairly and this put pressure on the government to pardon them.

Government The government was especially hard on trade unions because it wanted to protect the interests of wealthy landowners and other employers who had the vote. Ordinary working men were unable to vote and so their views were less important. The government was also fearful of riot or revolution and so disliked groups of workers cooperating.

Revision task

Make a concept map that helps to summarise the story of the Tolpuddle Martyrs. You can include pictures to help make this more memorable.

Eliminate irrelevance

Below is an exam-style question.

Explain why the Tolpuddle Martyrs were punished so harshly in the nineteenth century. (12 marks)

1. Below is a paragraph which is part of an answer to the above question. Some parts of the answer are not relevant to the question being asked. Draw a line through any irrelevant information that does not directly help to answer the question.

2. Add one more reason of your own that helps to answer the question.

The Tolpuddle Martyrs were six agricultural labourers from the small Dorset village of Tolpuddle. Their wages had fallen and in 1833 were cut even further. Therefore, the six men set up a union, the Friendly Society of Agricultural Labourers. Each man was blindfolded and swore an oath of secrecy and support for the union. The men were arrested using a law against secret oaths and were sentenced to seven years' transportation in Australia. This was intended to deter other workers from organising themselves in trade unions as this was seen as a threat to the interests of landowners and employers. Unlike landowners and employers, ordinary working men were unable to vote and so their interests were less important.

3 The nature of law enforcement and punishment (1)

For hundreds of years, policing had been the responsibility of local people. However, the Metropolitan Police Act of 1829 introduced 3200 professional and full-time policemen to London and opened the way for police forces across the country.

3.1 The Fielding brothers and the Bow Street Runners

Home Secretary **Robert Peel** was not the first to improve policing in the capital. London magistrates Henry and John Fielding took over Bow Street Magistrates' Court in 1748 and took the following steps:

- Introduced a horse patrol to stop highwaymen around London.
- Established a newspaper, *The Hue and Cry*, to share information on crime and criminals across the country.
- Created the Bow Street Runners, a team of thief-takers who patrolled the streets of London in the evenings, investigated crimes and gave evidence in court.

> **Key individual**
>
> **Robert Peel** As Home Secretary, Peel was responsible for the Metropolitan Police Act. He also played significant roles in ending the Bloody Code (see page 22) and in the growing use of prisons (see pages 30–1).

3.2 Case study: Robert Peel and the Metropolitan Police Force

Traditionally, people had feared the cost of a police force and worried that the government might use it to limit people's freedoms. However, Peel's reforms were successful for the following reasons:

Increased taxation	Increasing crime
Government was more involved in people's lives. The war with France (1803–15) had forced it to raise more money through taxes.	The crime rate had risen quite sharply in the years following the French wars when unemployment was a problem.
Local authorities were also given powers to raise taxes that could help pay for a police force.	There was public fear that crime, especially violent crime, was out of control.
Fear of protest	**Growth of towns**
High food prices and unemployment led to many protests after 1815. The government feared revolution as a real possibility.	The growth of towns made constables and watchmen less effective. There were too many people, crammed into closely packed houses and streets. This was especially serious in London.
The role of Peel	
Peel used statistics to demonstrate rising crime. He reassured fellow politicians that a police force was no threat to freedom and this persuaded them to vote for the Act.	

3.3 The development of policing after 1829

At first, the police were regarded with suspicion. However, by the 1850s attitudes were more supportive and continued to improve.

- **1835:** Towns could establish their own police force.
- **1839:** Counties could establish their own police force. Bow Street Runners merged with the Metropolitan Police.
- **1842:** Metropolitan Police set up the first detective force to investigate and solve crimes.
- **1856:** Compulsory for all towns and counties to have police forces.
- **1878:** Metropolitan Police detective force became the Criminal Investigation Department (CID). In following years other forces established their own CID.
- **1884:** 39,000 policemen in Britain in over 200 separate forces.

 Making comparisons

Look at the exam-style questions below and the two answers. Which answer is better for comparing the key features? Why?

Explain one way policing methods in England c.1000–c.1500 were different from policing methods in the nineteenth century. (4 marks)

> Policing in England c.1500–c.1700 used methods such as the constable and the hue and cry. These were based around the local community working together to catch criminals. Moreover, constables were unpaid and part time. By the nineteenth century things had changed and in 1829 the government set up and paid for the first ever police force in London. It was now the job of the police to catch criminals.

> Policing in England c.1500–c.1700 was different from policing in the nineteenth century because there was no full-time professional police force before 1829.

4 The nature of law enforcement and punishment (2)

4.1 The abolition of the Bloody Code

The Bloody Code was abolished by the reforms of Sir Robert Peel in the 1820s.
Crime was increasing and the system was failing for the following reasons:

Juries were not convicting.	• Juries were often unwilling to convict as execution was seen as too harsh for many offences. Therefore, some guilty criminals were found innocent and so escaped justice.
Public executions were not working.	• Large crowds made it hard to keep order and criminals could sometimes escape. There was a risk of riot when offenders were executed for minor crimes. • Executions were no longer a deterrent. Many saw them as cheap entertainment and drunkenness was common. The large crowds created opportunities for further crime such as pickpocketing.
Ideas about punishment were changing.	• Some began to argue that punishments should aim to **reform** criminals. • Alternatives to capital punishment were being tried. Transportation had emerged as the main alternative to executing criminals.

4.2 Transportation

Criminals were sent to Australia and made to work. Those committing further
offences were flogged or sent to more distant settlements. Lawmakers hoped that
transportation would be a success.

Successes of transportation	Failures of transportation
Juries were more willing to convict criminals if the sentence was transportation and not execution.	The crime rate in Britain increased rather than fell after transportation began.
By the 1830s, Australia was firmly part of the British Empire.	By the 1830s, transportation cost half a million pounds every year – an enormous amount at the time.
	By the 1830s, wages in Australia were higher than in Britain. Therefore, transportation was more of an opportunity than a deterrent once prisoners had won a ticket of leave.
Many convicts with **tickets of leave** remained in Australia, becoming respected members of the community.	Many settlers protested against the 'dumping' of convicts in Australia. They wanted to end the idea that everyone there was a criminal.
	Transportation declined in the 1840s. Prisons were being used more widely (see below) and in 1868 transportation was ended, largely due to pressure from settlers.

4.3 Changes to prisons

The government started to use prisons as the main punishment for serious crimes.
Sir Robert Peel, influenced by the ideas of reformers **John Howard** and
Elizabeth Fry, improved conditions with the 1823 **Gaols** Act. Later changes
reflected debate over whether prisons should reform the inmates or provide as
harsh a deterrent as possible.

Privately run prisons before the 1823 Gaols Act

- Hardened criminals mixed with first-time offenders, women and children.
  Prisons were 'schools for crime'.
- **Warders** were unpaid so prisoners paid them for food, to see a doctor and
  even to be released. Wealthier inmates could afford perks such as better food
  while the poor relied on charities to pay their fees.
- Conditions were unhealthy and overcrowded. Disease killed hundreds.

Prisons after the 1823 Gaols Act

- Prisoners were separated. Female warders were introduced for women prisoners.
- Warders were paid wages so no longer charged fees.

> ### Key terms
>
> **Gaols** The old-fashioned word for prison.
>
> **Reform** The belief that criminals could be helped to lead more honest lives.
>
> **Tickets of leave** Early release for good behaviour.
>
> **Warders** Prison guard.

- Prisons became healthier with fresh water and drainage. All prisoners got proper food.
- Prisoners were given religious instruction and services.
- Magistrates inspected prisons in their area.

Separate system, 1830s onwards

- Prisoners spent most time alone in their cells. This encouraged inmates to reflect on their crimes rather than be influenced by other criminals.
- Religious services encouraged prisoners to lead honest lives.
- Prisoners had to work in their cells so they might get honest jobs when released.

Silent system, 1860s onwards

- Prisoners were kept silent at all times or faced punishment such as a diet of bread and water.
- Food was 'hard fare' – adequate but the same every day.
- Prisoners did 'hard labour' – physically demanding work for twelve hours a day.
- Prisoners slept on hard wooden boards instead of traditional hammocks

4.4 Case study: Pentonville and the separate system

Pentonville was built in 1842 and designed using the latest technology to isolate prisoners.

- The walls were thick to stop prisoners communicating between their small cells.
- Each prisoner had a basin, piped water and toilet to ensure they had no need to leave their cell. The building had modern ventilation and heating systems.
- Prisoners wore facemasks during exercise to prevent them seeing other inmates. During religious instruction, the prisoners sat in individual cubicles in silence.

In the first eight years at Pentonville, 22 prisoners went mad, 26 had nervous breakdowns and three killed themselves. This was no doubt the result of solitary confinement and the lack of human contact.

 Analysing factors

You need to understand the role that factors had on the development of prisons in the eighteenth and nineteenth centuries.

Make a copy of the concentric circles. Choose the factors in the box that you think influenced the development of prisons. Next, decide where to write the factors on the diagram to show the importance of their roles. The middle circle is the most important and the least important is the outer circle. Add annotations around the diagram to explain your thinking.

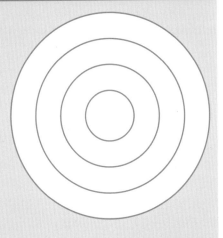

FACTORS

- government
- individuals
- attitudes in society
- the Church (and religious beliefs)
- science and technology.

Key individuals

Elizabeth Fry Visited women in Newgate prison and was horrified at the overcrowded conditions and the exploitation of women prisoners by the male warders. Her ideas influenced the 1823 Gaols Act.

John Howard In 1777 he wrote *The State of Prison in England and Wales*. He strongly attacked the fees prisoners had to pay. He proposed healthier accommodation, the separation of prisoners, a decent diet and better warders. During his lifetime, Howard was criticised as too lenient but after his death his ideas became influential.

Key factors

Government The government collected higher taxes, which they used to take over and improve private prisons and to construct expensive new prisons such as Pentonville.

Individuals Peel pushed through the reforms to prisons and was influenced by Fry and Howard.

Religious ideas Fry was a Quaker. Quakers believe that there is something of God in everyone, and so it follows that they can be reformed. Other reformers were also influenced by their Christian faith.

c.1900–present: Crime and punishment in modern Britain

Since 1900, social, cultural and technological developments have led to changing definitions of crime, as well as a revolution in law enforcement. Moreover, capital punishment was finally ended.

1 Nature and changing definitions of criminal activity

REVISED

1.1 New crimes and old

The twentieth century was an era of two world wars, economic boom and bust, and tremendous technological advances. It is no wonder that old crimes have developed and new crimes appeared.

Car crime	• Car ownership was very low in 1900. Today car theft has become one of the largest categories of crime. • The driving test, road tax and insurance were all introduced in the 1930s. Today, motoring offences absorb a huge amount of police time.
Cybercrime	• Fraudsters trick people into handing over important details or passwords. Money is then stolen from their bank accounts. • The internet has made it easier to illegally copy music and films. • Hacking has become a criminal offence.
Theft, burglary and shoplifting	• Petty theft is still the most common type of crime. • Today, drug addiction frequently leads to theft as addicts steal to fund their habit. • Shoplifting became established in the second half of the century, as more shops placed goods on display. This made shoplifting easier and more tempting.
Terrorism	• The IRA (Irish Republican Army) carried out bomb attacks on buildings in Britain between the 1970s and 1990s. • More recently, far-right extremists have committed acts of terror.
Violent crime and sexual offences	• Violent crimes and sexual offences both increased in the later twentieth century, partly due to an increased willingness of victims to report offences. • New laws better protect people from domestic violence and intimidation. • New laws better protect women from sexual abuse within a marriage.
Murder	• The number of murders increased after 1900, but not as quickly as other crimes. • The majority of murderers know the victim and have never committed a serious offence before. Most murders are unplanned and in the heat of the moment.
Hate crimes	• In 2007, the government introduced a new law covering 'hate crimes'. Hate crimes range from criminal damage and vandalism through to harassment or physical assault. Victims are targeted for their race, sexual orientation, religion or disability. • The most common hate crimes have racist motives but in recent years, the number of religiously motivated hate crimes has grown.
Smuggling	• With millions of people travelling in and out of the country by air, land and sea, smuggling is much harder to prevent. • Legal items such as tobacco and alcohol are smuggled into the country in huge quantities every day. There is big public demand as smuggled alcohol and tobacco are much cheaper than in the shops. • Demand for illegal drugs has continued to rise in the last 40 years and consequently the illegal drug business has become a multi-billion-pound industry. • Tougher immigration controls and conflict in different parts of the world have led to an increase in people trafficking. Those who might otherwise not be allowed to enter Britain pay to be smuggled into the country. Many are then exploited by criminal gangs.

1.2 Case study: The treatment of conscientious objectors in the First and Second World Wars

Conscription was introduced during the First and Second World Wars. This law required men aged between 18 and 41 to join the armed forces. Conscientious objectors (COs) were those thousands of men who refused to take part on moral or religious grounds.

During the Second World War, there was some softening in the government's response. It would have seemed hypocritical to persecute a minority group like COs when the country was fighting against the brutality of the Nazis. However, public attitudes towards COs remained negative.

War	Government response to COs	Public attitudes to COs
First World War (1914–18)	• COs faced a local tribunal (special court). These were often unsympathetic and included retired soldiers. • Some COs given work vital to the war effort. Others took non-fighting roles at the front line, which could be incredibly dangerous. • Those who refused to support the war in any way were imprisoned. They faced hard labour and solitary confinement. 73 COs died. • Banned COs from voting until 1926.	• Seen as cowards and traitors. Some physical attacks. • Many were sacked from their jobs. • Newspapers were critical.
Second World War (1939–45)	• Tribunals were more balanced and no longer included ex-soldiers. • A greater effort was made to give COs alternative work such as farming or munitions that were vital to the war effort. • COs sent to prison only as a last resort.	

✎ Change and continuity

Draw your own copy of the Venn diagram and write the following offences in the corresponding part of the circles:

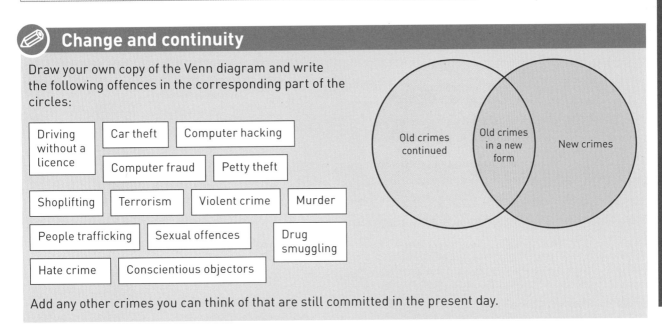

Driving without a licence   Car theft   Computer hacking

Computer fraud   Petty theft

Shoplifting   Terrorism   Violent crime   Murder

People trafficking   Sexual offences   Drug smuggling

Hate crime   Conscientious objectors

Add any other crimes you can think of that are still committed in the present day.

✎ Analysing factors

Which of the following factors do you think have had the biggest effect on the development of crimes in the twentieth century? Explain your reasons.

- government
- individuals
- attitudes in society
- The Church (and religious beliefs)
- science and technology.

2 The nature of law enforcement and punishment (1)

The powers of the police to question, search or arrest suspects have changed little since 1900. However, there have been some important changes that have influenced the way officers carry out their duties.

2.1 Increased specialisation in the police force

Since 1947, police officers are expected to undergo fourteen weeks of basic training at the National Police College. Their training continues with a more experienced officer once they first begin their duties.

Crime has become more varied and complex (see page 32). Therefore, the police use specialist units including the Fraud Squad, Drugs Squad, dog-handlers, counter-terrorist squads, cybercrime units and others. Specialist firearms officers are used when there is a high level of threat.

2.2 The impact of science and technology on policing

- Since 1901, fingerprints and analysis of blood samples have been used to identify suspects. More recently, DNA samples have been successfully used as evidence.
- The Police National Computer collects together databases including fingerprints, motor vehicles and missing person details.
- Automatic Number Plate Recognition (ANPR) cameras read registrations and identify vehicles of interest. Police can stop a vehicle, search it and make arrests.
- Motor vehicles have improved response speed. Police helicopters track suspects and support officers on the ground. Two-way radios allow instant communication with other officers and headquarters.

2.3 Crime prevention and community relations

The police advise people on crime prevention, such as fitting locks and alarms to property and vehicles. In 1982, the Neighbourhood Watch began. Members of the community report suspicious behaviour which police can follow up. CCTV and other security recordings are used to prevent crime and identify suspects.

There has been a move back towards police officers walking or cycling a 'beat'. Local forces have increased numbers of police officers and **PCSOs** on patrol in an attempt to improve community relations in certain neighbourhoods.

The police have also attempted to recruit more ethnic minorities and women into the force. Although numbers have greatly increased, the proportion of such officers remains low. This had led to criticism that the police force has remained largely male and overwhelmingly white in comparison to rest of the population.

Key term

PCSO Police Community Support Officer – a uniformed civilian member of police support staff. Usually patrols a beat and interacts with the public, while also offering assistance to police officers at crime scenes and major events.

Revision task

Use the information on this page to write ten knowledge-based quiz questions on changes to law enforcement c.1900–present. Make sure that you also record the answers somewhere. Questions could be multiple choice, multiple select, true or false, or even require short sentences as answers. Just by composing these questions you are already revising key content. Swap your questions with someone else in your class. Have a go at their quiz and then mark each other's answers.

Organising knowledge

Use your knowledge of this topic to fill in the final column of the table below. This will help summarise the development of the modern police force.

	Policing in 1900	Policing today
Organisation	• Around 200 local police forces – all run differently. • Little cooperation between forces.	
Training	• Military drill the only training. • All police officers were male. • Low-quality and poorly paid recruits.	
Patrol	• Officers walked a 'beat' of up to twenty miles a day.	
Equipment	• Whistle to call for help. • Wooden truncheon. • Pistols locked up at police station for emergencies.	
Crime investigation tools	• Eyes and ears of the officer. • Witness statements.	
Record keeping	• Local record-keeping was poor. • No national record of criminals.	

Analysing factors

1 Summarise how the following factors have influenced modern policing:
- government

_____

_____

_____

- attitudes in society

_____

_____

_____

_____

_____

- science and technology

_____

_____

_____

_____

_____

2 Explain which has had the biggest influence overall

_____

_____

_____

_____

_____

3 The nature of law enforcement and punishment (2)

3.1 The abolition of the death penalty

Since the middle ages, the ultimate punishment was always the death penalty. However, in 1965 capital punishment was finally abolished. There were a number of reasons for this:

A gradual decline in executions	• Public hangings had been abolished in 1868 and since then the government had gradually reduced the number of crimes carrying the death penalty.
The impact of the Second World War	• Following the Second World War (1939–45) and the horrors of the Holocaust, there was a growing feeling that execution was un-Christian and barbaric. Execution now seemed wrong, the kind of action one associated with Hitler's Germany rather than Britain.
Miscarriages of justice	• Two well-publicised cases helped to turn the argument in favour of abolition. The first was the case of Timothy Evans, who was wrongly hanged in March 1950. The second was the case of Derek Bentley, executed in 1953. Both cases showed that mistakes could be made and sometimes the wrong person was executed.
Other reasons	• Other European countries had abolished capital punishment without a noticeable increase in crime • Most murders are committed on the spur of the moment and without thinking. Therefore, capital punishment does not deter them.

3.2 Case study: Derek Bentley

Derek Bentley had severe learning difficulties. He found it hard to do even basic jobs and was easily led. In November 1952, Bentley, along with his sixteen-year-old companion, Chris Craig, were caught burgling a warehouse in London. Craig was carrying a gun.

The police arrived while Bentley and Craig were on the roof. Detective Sergeant Fairfax managed to arrest Bentley and asked Craig to hand over the gun. At this point Bentley shouted, 'Let him have it, Chris.' Craig fired at Fairfax, injuring him in the shoulder. However, Bentley did nothing and made no attempt to escape. More officers climbed onto the roof and PC Sidney Miles was shot and killed.

Bentley and Craig were *both* charged with murder. Craig was under eighteen so too young to hang, but Bentley faced execution if found guilty. Bentley and Craig denied that Bentley ever said, 'Let him have it.' Even if he had said it, Bentley's lawyer argued, he could have meant 'hand over the gun'.

There was controversy over whether Bentley was fit to stand trial given his low intelligence. Despite not firing the fatal shot, Bentley was found guilty and sentenced to death, although the jury asked for mercy for him. There was huge public outcry at the result and this further undermined the use of the death penalty.

Key term

Non-custodial
An alternative sentence to being locked up in prison.

Revision task

Summarise the following:

- reasons for the abolition of the death penalty
- the Derek Bentley case
- changes to prisons
- open prisons
- treatment of young offenders
- non-custodial punishments.

Answers and quick quizzes at **www.hoddereducation.co.uk/myrevisionnotes**

3.3 Changes to prisons and non-custodial punishments

A prison sentence keeps criminals off the street and demonstrates to the public that the government is being tough on crime. However, there are several problems with prison as a punishment:

- High rates of recidivism (prisoners reoffending) after release.
- Younger prisoners can learn from older criminals or develop drug addictions, which result in further crime when they are released.
- Prison is expensive. Inmates have to be housed and fed. Staff must be paid and prisoners' families need financial support if they lose the main breadwinner.
- Prison does not deal with the social or personal problems that caused the inmate to commit a crime.

	Changes since 1900
Prison	• Solitary confinement was ended and prisoners are allowed to associate with each other. Convict uniforms were abolished, as was the shaved hairstyle prisoners wore. • Diet, heating and conditions in the cells were improved gradually and more visits were allowed. • Teachers were employed in prisons to help inmates have a better chance of finding work when released. • Most recently, reduced budgets and difficulties in recruiting have led to fewer staff looking after more prisoners in overcrowded prisons. Consequently, prisoners spend much longer in their cells. • There has been an increase in drug use and the number of serious assaults in prison.
Open prisons	• The first open prison was built in 1933. Rules in open prisons are more relaxed. • Prisoners are allowed to leave the grounds to work in order to help prepare them for ordinary life in the community. The use of open prisons was expanded and continues today.
Treatment of young offenders	• Parents can be fined if their children are not under control. Social services can remove children from families. • Youth Courts work with agencies such as the police, school, social workers and probation officers. The aim is to prevent the young person settling into a life of crime. • Non-custodial methods such as tagging and curfews are used to monitor offenders' movements and courts can order youngsters to attend counselling. • Custody is a last resort. Offenders under eighteen can be held in a secure children's home, a secure training centre or a young offenders' institution. These have many of the same rules as prisons.
Non-custodial punishments	• 1967: suspended sentences introduced. Offenders who do not reoffend can avoid prison. • 1972: Community Service Orders introduced. Offenders do 40–300 hours' unpaid work in the community instead of being locked up. • 1990s: electronic tags were introduced. These track an offender's location. Courts and police can impose restrictions on the offender's movements.

Memory map

Create a concept map to summarise the changes to punishment: c.1900–present. Add to the map using the information on these two pages. Use key words or phrases. Do not write in full sentences. You could also add some small drawings to help you remember.

The abolition of the death penalty — CHANGES TO PUNISHMENT c.1900–PRESENT — Changes to prisons and non-custodial punishments

Part 2 Whitechapel, c.1870–c.1900: crime, policing and the inner city

In this historic environment unit you will focus on just one historic site: Whitechapel, c1870–1900. Your knowledge of nineteenth-century policing will be useful but you will also be expected to look closely at contemporary sources.

1 The context of Whitechapel

Whitechapel is an area of London's East End. In our period, it was an area of extreme poverty – a place where lots of different types of people lived, many of whom were poor due to a lack of reliable employment.

1.1 Housing in Whitechapel

Conditions	Attempts to improve housing
• Houses in **rookeries** were divided into apartments so more people could be packed in. Shared outside toilets soon became unsanitary. This meant cheaper rents but conditions were poor. • The poorest lived in the estimated 200 lodging or 'doss' houses, spending one or two nights in a place, before trying to earn enough money to eat and for the cost of their next night's 'doss'. • Some lodging houses operated in three eight-hour shifts, so that three people might sleep in one bed each day. Not surprisingly, these were very unhygienic.	Attempts were made to improve housing and the government provided funds for slum clearance. The rookery near Royal Mint Street was replaced with flats when the Peabody Estate opened in 1881. Each of the 287 separate flats offered improved ventilation, unplastered walls that could not be infested by lice, and shared bathrooms and kitchens. However, rents were too high for most locals, and tenants who got behind with their rent were thrown out. Therefore, improvements like these caused more overcrowding elsewhere as the poorest people looked for rents they actually could afford.

Key terms

Rookeries Slum areas of terribly overcrowded and filthy housing.

Sweatshop A workshop, often making clothes or shoes, where people were paid low wages (often only receiving a small sum for each item they finished).

1.2 Work and workhouses in Whitechapel

Many Whitechapel residents worked in small, dark, overcrowded and dusty **sweatshops** in trades such as shoemaking, tailoring and making matches. Hours were very long and wages were low.

Others worked as labourers in railway construction or in the London docks. However, the amount of paid work varied from day to day and many families could not rely on a steady income.

Those unable to afford a lodging house for the night, or who were too young, too old or too unwell to work, could go to the workhouse. The Whitechapel Workhouse was at South Grove, to the east, just off Mile End Road. This was a last resort because the rules in workhouses were very strict and families were kept apart. Inmates were expected to earn their bed for the night by doing hard labour.

Without regular or well-paid employment, it was inevitable that a number of Whitechapel's inhabitants would turn to crime in order to avoid the workhouse.

Exam tip

You need to be able to explain the impact that the context of Whitechapel had on crime and policing.

Revision task

Make a concept map that helps to summarise the context of Whitechapel. You can include pictures to help make this more memorable.

You're the examiner

Below is an exam-style question.

Describe two features of work in the Whitechapel district in the late nineteenth century. (4 marks)

1 Below are a mark scheme and an answer to this question. Read the answer and the mark scheme. Decide how many marks it would get. Write the mark along with a justification for your choice below.

Mark scheme

Award 1 mark for each valid feature identified up to maximum of two features. The second mark should be awarded for supporting features.

> Work in Whitechapel was often poorly rewarded. Many people worked very long hours in sweatshops where the wages were low and the hours long.

Mark ☐   Reason _____

_____

2 Now suggest what the student has to do to achieve a higher level.

3 Write an answer that would achieve more marks

_____
_____
_____
_____

Spot the mistakes

Describe two features of attempts to improve housing in Whitechapel. (4 marks)

The paragraph below is an answer to the question above. However, it is full of factual mistakes. Once you have identified the mistakes, rewrite the paragraph to include accurate points and supporting details.

> The Peabody Estates were opened in 1851 to replace the rookeries near Royal Mint Avenue. The flats offered improved ventilation, lice-free walls and proper shared bathrooms and kitchens. The rents were too high for most locals and those who could not keep up with their payments were thrown out. This reduced overcrowding in other areas.

_____
_____
_____
_____
_____
_____

2 Tensions in Whitechapel

The residents of Whitechapel faced increasing competition for housing and employment with immigrants from Ireland and eastern Europe. This caused various tensions within the community. When the Ripper murders began (see page 46), some members of the press and the public argued that the killer must be a foreigner as no Englishman would be capable of such barbaric acts.

2.1 Irish immigration

Since the early nineteenth century, young Irish men had been coming to England to make a living working as labourers on canals, roads and railways. Large numbers settled in Whitechapel due to the cheap lodgings and closeness to the docks. They were often hard drinking and this could lead to violence, causing tension with the rest of the community.

The Irish were targets of prejudice because of their Catholic religion, but also because of the rise in 'Fenian' Irish Nationalism. Ireland was ruled by Britain, but many Irish people wanted independence. In 1884, the Fenians began a bombing campaign. Although only a few people were hurt, public opinion stereotyped the Irish as violent criminals and potential terrorists.

2.2 Eastern European Jewish immigration

After 1881, Russian Jewish people came to England in large numbers because they were persecuted in Russia following the assassination of Tsar Alexander II. Around 30,000 arrived in London between 1881 and 1891.

Jewish immigrants generally found it harder to integrate than Irish people, partly because of language barriers, but also because of cultural and religious differences. Many Jewish immigrants spoke only **Yiddish** and so ended up working for more established Jewish employers, often in sweatshops. This meant that Jewish workers were often quite separate from the wider community and therefore a target for prejudice.

2.3 The growth of anarchism and socialism

There were fears that immigrants were bringing dangerous political views with them. There had been several attempted assassinations and bomb attacks in Europe, carried out by anarchists. The idea of **anarchism** was developed by Russian revolutionaries, and therefore the authorities and the public were suspicious of Jewish immigrants from eastern Europe.

Some Jewish immigrants did bring revolutionary political beliefs and set up **socialist** organisations and newspapers. There were strikes and demonstrations, usually demanding shorter working hours and better pay in sweatshop industries. The authorities feared socialist movements, which they felt could encourage unrest and even revolution. Therefore, the police in Whitechapel were often busy dealing with such groups.

> ### Key terms
>
> **Anarchism** A revolutionary political idea which said that people would be better off without government and without laws.
>
> **Fenians** Those wanting an independent Ireland free from British rule.
>
> **Socialism** A political and economic system in which property and resources are owned or controlled by the state.
>
> **Yiddish** A language used by Jewish people in central and eastern Europe.

Utility question

Look at the two sources, the exam-style question and the two answers below. Which answer is the better answer to the question and why? You could look at page 50 for guidance on how to answer the utility question to help you make your own judgement.

SOURCE A

From a Letter to the Home Office from the Superintendent of Whitechapel Division, 1904.

Bills and circulars [leaflets] in this language are distributed and posted all over the division, but police know nothing of their [meaning]. As it is known that a number of these people are members of Continental Revolutionary Societies it would be very desirable to have members of the service who could speak this language.

Study Sources A and B. How useful are sources A and B for an enquiry into tensions caused by immigration in Whitechapel? Explain your answer, using Sources A and B and your own knowledge of the historical context. (8 marks)

SOURCE B

From Illustrated Police News. This image was taken from the front page in 1888, showing how those living outside Whitechapel saw the immigrant communities who lived there.

ANSWER 1

Source A is useful for this enquiry because it tells us about some of the activities of revolutionary groups of immigrants in Whitechapel. Source B is useful because it shows us that immigrants in Whitechapel were seen as rough sorts.

ANSWER 2

Source A is useful because it tells us about some of the activities of revolutionary groups of immigrants in Whitechapel. From my own knowledge, I know these groups were feared by the authorities who thought they caused unrest, strikes and even possible revolution. Secondly, it mentions the police not understanding the language used in the bills and circulars. I know that this relates to Yiddish, a language spoken by Jewish immigrants. This is useful because I know that language barriers made it harder for some Jewish people to integrate with the wider community in Whitechapel. The fact that Source A is a letter to the Home Secretary suggests that the activities of such groups were taken seriously by the government.

Source B is useful because it shows us that immigrants in Whitechapel were seen as rough sorts by some. This reflects what I know about attitudes towards immigrants, especially Irish navvies, who had reputation for drunkenness and violence. However, it comes from a popular news-sheet that was produced to sell copies and entertain its readers. It might be exaggerating the roughness of immigrants for effect and may not accurately reflect what how people living in Whitechapel felt towards them.

Which answer is better? [ ]   Why? _____

3 The organisation of policing in Whitechapel

3.1 H Division

The Metropolitan Police was split up into different 'divisions' – each was responsible for policing a different area of London. Whitechapel came under H Division.

At its peak during 1888, there were only around 575 police officers in H Division – meaning there was one policeman for every 300 people in Whitechapel. Although better than in some parts of the capital, it was hardly enough men considering the difficulties that Whitechapel faced.

3.2 Key features that made policing Whitechapel so difficult

Rookeries and lodging houses

- The narrow streets and alleys of rookeries provided places for criminals to operate and hide from the law.
- Lodging houses attracted people moving through Whitechapel, like sailors, who had no ties to the community. Such people cared less about engaging in criminal behaviours than more permanent residents.
- Cheap accommodation often attracted criminals, drunk and disorderly individuals and sex workers.
- Cramped conditions caused tensions and opportunities for petty theft.

Problems caused by alcohol

- Drinking was one way of coping with the difficulties of life in Whitechapel, and addiction to alcohol was responsible for some turning to crime after losing their jobs.
- Drinking made people vulnerable. All of Jack the Ripper's (see page 46) victims were people suffering from alcohol addiction, and were probably drunk when attacked. There are plenty of other examples of victims being robbed while drunk.
- Alcohol reduced people's inhibitions and affected their judgement. This could lead to people making the wrong choices and committing crimes. It also caused disagreements to escalate into violence.
- The very high number of pubs and gin-palaces in Whitechapel made these problems more common as alcohol was so cheaply available.

Problems associated with sex work

- By 1888, there were an estimated 1200 sex workers in Whitechapel. While sex work was not illegal it was viewed as a serious social problem.
- Sex work was sometimes linked to organised crime, and sex workers themselves sometimes became involved in crimes such as petty theft.
- Sex work sometimes made women more vulnerable to misogynistic attacks and sexual violence.

Gangs and protection rackets

- Criminal gangs such as the Bessarabian Tigers and the Odessians demanded protection money from small businesses. Those refusing to pay might have their property destroyed or even be harmed themselves.
- People feared speaking out against the gangs and so it was difficult for the police to collect enough evidence to prosecute them.

Antisemitism and xenophobia

- There were antisemitic attacks on Jewish people and clumsy attempts by Christians to convert them. This created tensions that the police had to spend time dealing with.

- Recently arrived Jewish immigrants were unlikely to go to the police if they were victims of crime, because they had been persecuted by the police in their homelands. Many newly arrived Jewish immigrants spoke only Yiddish, which complicated matters further.

- During the Ripper case, hostility towards Irish and Jewish immigrants increased as foreigners were blamed for the murders. Police reinforcements were sent to Whitechapel to help prevent further unrest.

Exam tip

The examiner wants you to be able to explain how the environment in Whitechapel created more crime and made policing the area so difficult.

Organising knowledge

1 It is important to be able to explain rather than simply describe the key features that made policing Whitechapel so difficult. Use the list below, and any others you can think of, to add crimes that may have resulted from each feature.

Feature of Whitechapel	Possible resultant crimes
Rookeries and lodging houses.	
Problems caused by alcohol.	
Problems associated with sex work.	
Gangs and protection rackets.	
Antisemitism and xenophobia.	

Petty theft	Domestic violence	Drunk and disorderly conduct	Sexual offences	Murder	Extortion	Assault

2 The key features of Whitechapel sometimes combined to make life harder for the police. We have begun to show how some features are linked below. Make your own copy of the diagram, draw your own links and add explanations.

Problems associated with sex work ←————————————→ **Problems caused by alcohol**

Some women suffering from alcohol addiction who had lost their jobs turned to sex work. Drunkenness made them even more vulnerable

Rookeries and lodging houses

Gangs and protection rackets   **Antisemitism and xenophobia**

Complete the answer

Below are an exam-style question and an answer. The answer identifies two features, but does not develop them with any supporting knowledge. Annotate the answer to complete it by adding the support.

Describe two features of the effect of alcohol on crime in Whitechapel. (4 marks)

Drink made people more vulnerable in Whitechapel. Drunkenness affected their judgements.

4 The workings of the Metropolitan Police

4.1 Recruitment

Recruits were chosen from outside London, because they were thought to be bigger and healthier than city dwellers. This meant they would be better able to patrol their 'beat' and be physically up to the job of arresting criminals. Character was important – honest men who could take orders and not break the rules were desirable.

Policing offered steady employment at a time when many other jobs were temporary. Those officers who stayed in the job long enough could expect decent promotion prospects and a good pension.

4.2 The role of the beat constable

The role of the beat constable was to prevent crime by being an obvious presence, and to arrest those caught committing a crime. The beat was a specific route that each constable would have to patrol, usually alone.

Uniform and equipment	The beat routine
The uniform was meant to stand out in the crowd: • blue-black woollen trousers and jacket, with shiny buttons • a specially designed helmet to deflect a downward blow to the side. A truncheon was carried for protection and handcuffs for making arrests. An oil-fired lantern provided both light and warmth.	The constable was expected to reach certain places at specific times so that his sergeant could meet or contact him when necessary. The day beat lasted about half an hour. At night, the beats were walked every fifteen minutes. Criminals could observe a constable's route, making it possible to choose their moments to commit crimes. Constables sometimes reversed their beat to guard against this. Officers were expected to know the pubs, shops and other businesses, as well as the alleyways, yards and squares that led off their beat. After a month, a policeman would be moved to another beat. This was to prevent corruption between officers and locals.

4.3 The role of the Criminal Investigation Department (CID)

The first detective force had been set up in 1842 but was ineffective. More detectives were recruited in 1870 but they did not perform well. There were cases of mistaken identity which led to arrests of the wrong person. After a corruption scandal in 1877, the CID was set up.

The detective's main job was to observe and gather information. Detectives began to use photography (see page 46), but there was no reliable way of taking fingerprints and no forensics. Most evidence was gathered from interviews, witness statements or tips from informants.

4.4 The Home Secretary and Sir Charles Warren

Sir Charles Warren became Metropolitan Police Commissioner in 1886. Although the Metropolitan Police was paid for by local London authorities, it was controlled by the Home Secretary.

Commissioner Warren increased military drill and tightened up the rules for recruitment. He also brought more ex-soldiers into the force. In 1887, Warren was criticised for using too much force to control a demonstration in Trafalgar Square. The press and the public reacted angrily, concerned that the force was becoming an army which could be used to control the people.

Further criticism of Warren followed in late 1888, when the Ripper murders began in Whitechapel (see page 46). The killer appeared to run rings round the police, who looked incapable of catching him. In an angry exchange of letters with the Home Secretary, Warren felt forced to resign. The breakdown in the relationship between the Commissioner and the Home Secretary further undermined confidence in the Metropolitan Police.

Revision task

Summarise the workings of the Metropolitan Police:

- recruitment
- the beat constable
- CID
- the Home Secretary and Commissioner.

Eliminate irrelevance

Below is an exam-style question:

Describe two features of recruitment to the Metropolitan Police. (4 marks)

Below is an answer to this question. Read the answer and identify the parts that are not directly relevant to the question. Draw a line through the information that is irrelevant and justify your deletions in the margin.

> The Metropolitan Police was split up into different 'divisions' – each was responsible for policing a different area of London. Most officers in each division were beat constables who were an obvious presence on the streets. Recruits usually came from the countryside because they were thought to be strong and healthy enough to walk a beat and arrest criminals. They carried truncheons and handcuffs to help them in their daily duties and wore a noticeable blue uniform. Furthermore, policing offered the chance of a decent career and steady employment. Those who stayed in the force could expect a pension and good chances of promotion. Unlike other police forces, the Metropolitan Police was under the direct control of the Home Secretary.

Complete the answer

Below is an exam-style question:

Describe two features of the beat constable. (4 marks)

Below is a paragraph which attempts to answer the above question. The answer identifies two features, but does not develop them with any supporting knowledge. Annotate the answer with the necessary supporting detail.

> The beat constable patrolled a beat. They were expected to have some local knowledge.

5 Investigative policing in Whitechapel

Between 31 August and 9 November 1888, five women were murdered in similar and gruesome ways. The killer was nicknamed 'Jack the Ripper'. The case shines a light on investigative policing in Whitechapel and the challenges faced.

5.1 The Ripper murders

Mary Nichols (31 August).	Found in Bucks Row. Throat cut and abdomen cut open.
Annie Chapman (8 September).	Found near Hanbury Street. Throat cut following strangulation. Partially disemboweled.
Elizabeth Stride and Catherine Eddowes (30 September).	Stride found at Dutfield's Yard and Eddowes at Mitre Square. Stride's throat was cut. Killer was perhaps interrupted as no further injuries. Eddowes' face was mutilated and she was disembowelled.
Mary Kelly (9 November).	Found in her room. Terrible injuries, body parts removed and spread around.

5.2 Police investigative techniques

There were no forensic techniques available to help catch the killer. Fingerprinting was still twelve years away and scientists could not even distinguish different types of blood. Instead they relied on:

- **Autopsy:** all the Ripper's victims had autopsies, the details of which were given to the police. From the start, the police thought that they were looking for a left-handed murderer, from the way that the bodies were injured. The cuts also suggested a measure of skill and basic knowledge of anatomy.
- **Photography:** photos were taken of bodies before and after a post-mortem. These were used more to identify the victim rather than to help solve the crime.
- **Sketches:** the City of London Police used drawings of Mitre Square, and the doctor called to Catherine Eddowes' crime scene made a sketch of the position and condition of her body before she was moved.
- **Interviews:** the police visited houses and businesses in the areas around where the bodies were found. There was a full-scale search of lodging houses in Whitechapel, in the hope of finding evidence leading to the killer. Police questioned more than 2000 people, focusing on butchers and slaughter-men.

5.3 Media reporting

Newspapers presented the police as utterly useless. Moreover, sensationalist newspaper stories encouraged the nearly 300 hoax letters sent to the press and the police, from men claiming to be the Ripper. These wasted considerable police time.

The press also published unofficial sketches of 'foreign'-looking suspects. This increased tensions towards immigrants, especially Jewish people, even further.

5.4 Cooperation with other police forces

Catherine Eddowes was murdered in Mitre Square, within the City Police's territory. The City of London Police was a separate and independent force from the Metropolitan Police. On the night that Stride and Eddowes were killed some graffiti referring to Jewish people was found near the crime scene. Two City detectives saw the writing, and requested a photographer record it as evidence. Commissioner Warren (see page 44) decided that the risk of an antisemitic riot was too great to wait for a photographer to arrive. He made a copy of the writing,

Answers and quick quizzes at www.hoddereducation.co.uk/myrevisionnotes

and ordered the graffiti to be washed from the wall. This caused tensions between the Metropolitan and City forces, and criticism from the press that the investigation was incompetent. Warren probably did the right thing and most likely helped to prevent a riot but the investigation was further undermined.

Other divisions within the Metropolitan Police (see page 42) cooperated more fully and sent men to assist officers on the beat in Whitechapel.

5.5 The Whitechapel Vigilance Committee

George Lusk, a builder from Whitechapel, felt that not enough had been done to catch the killer and set up the Whitechapel Vigilance Committee. The Committee members were annoyed that the police had offered no rewards for information and so offered their own. Before long, Lusk started to receive hoax letters himself. The Committee also organised night patrols made up of volunteers. They were untrained, amateurish and noisy. This probably undermined the police investigation further.

 Organising knowledge

Make a concept map to summarise how the Ripper murders were investigated. Add notes to the outside using two different colours. Use one colour to summarise the things that helped the police investigation and use the other colour for the things that may have hindered its progress.

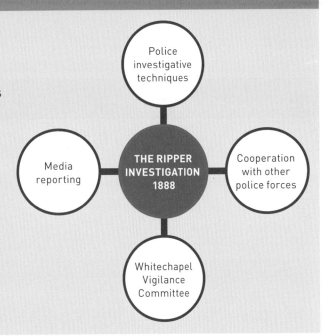

 Spot the mistakes

Describe two features of the treatment of the Ripper story by the newspapers. (4 marks)

The paragraph below is an answer to the question above. However, it is full of factual mistakes. Once you have identified the mistakes, rewrite the paragraph to include accurate points and supporting details.

Newspapers respected police efforts to catch the killer. Attention-grabbing newspaper stories resulted in nearly 100 hoax letters being sent to the press and the police, from men claiming to be the Ripper, and this helped the investigation. Secondly, the papers also printed their own unofficial sketches of rumoured suspects. These tended to be 'foreign'-looking. This increased tension towards immigrants, especially Irish people, even further.

Exam focus

Your History GCSE is made up of three exams:

- For Paper 1 you have one hour and 15 minutes to answer questions on a thematic study and historic environment, in your case Crime and punishment in Britain, c1000–present *and* Whitechapel, c1870–c1900: crime, policing and the inner city.
- In Paper 2 you have one hour and 45 minutes to answer questions on a period study and a British depth study.
- In Paper 3 you have one hour and 20 minutes to answer questions on a modern depth study.

For Paper 1 you have to answer the following types of questions. Each requires you to demonstrate different historical skills:

- **Question 1** is a key features question in which you have to describe two features and characteristics of the period.
- **Question 2** includes two sub-questions on a source enquiry which test your source analysis skills as well as your ability to frame a historical question.
- **Question 3** is a similarity or difference question in which you have to describe the similarity or difference in crime and punishment between two time periods.
- **Question 4** is a causation question which asks you to explain why something happened.
- **Questions 5 and 6** are analytical questions that ask you to evaluate change, continuity and significance in crime and punishment.

The table below gives a summary of the question types for Paper 1 and what you need to do.

Question number	Marks	Key words	You need to ...
1	4	Describe two features of	• Identify two features. • Add supporting information for each feature.
2(a)	8	How useful are Sources A and B for an enquiry into ... ? Explain your answer, using Sources A and B and your knowledge of the historical context.	• Ensure that you explain the value of the contents of each of the sources. • Explain how the provenance of each source affects the value of the contents. • Support your answer with your knowledge of the given topic.
2(b)	4	How could you follow up Source B to find out more about ... . In your answer you must give the question you would ask and the type of source you could use.	• Select a detail from Source B that could form the basis of a follow-up enquiry. • Write a question that is linked to this detail and enquiry. • Identify an appropriate source for the enquiry. • Explain how the source might help answer your follow-up question.
3	4	Explain one way in which ... were similar/different in the ... and ... centuries.	• Identify a similarity or difference. • Support the comparison with specific detail from both periods.
4	12	Explain why ... You may use the following in your answer: [two given points]. You **must** also use information of your own.	• Explain at least three causes – you can use the points in the question but must also use at least one point of your own. • Ensure that you focus the causes on the question.
5/6	20	'Statement'. How far do you agree? Explain your answer. You may use the following in your answer: [two given points]. You **must** also use information of your own.	• Ensure that you agree and disagree with the statement. • Use the given points and your own knowledge. • Ensure that you write a conclusion giving your final judgement on the question. • Remember that there are up to 4 marks for spelling, punctuation, grammar and the use of specialist terminology.

Answers and quick quizzes at **www.hoddereducation.co.uk/myrevisionnotes**

Question 1: Key features

Below is an example of a key features question which is worth 4 marks.

Describe two features of housing in Whitechapel between 1870 and 1900.

Feature 1: _____

_____

Feature 2: _____

_____

How to answer

You have to identify two features and add supporting information for each. For each of the two features you are given space to write. Remember you need to identify **two** different features.

Below is a sample answer to this key features question with comments around it.

Feature 1:

Housing in Whitechapel was very overcrowded. Houses in rookeries were often divided into apartments to pack more people in.

> The first feature is identified.

> Supporting information is added.

Feature 2:

There were also many unhygienic lodging houses. Some operated in three eight-hour shifts, so that three people might sleep in one bed each day.

> The second feature is identified.

> Supporting information is added.

✎ Complete the answer

Describe two features of the problems caused by alcohol in Whitechapel.

Here is the first part of an answer to this question.

Feature 1:

Drunkenness made people vulnerable to crime. All of Jack the Ripper's victims suffered from an addiction to alcohol, and may have been drunk when attacked.

1 Highlight the following:
- ● Where the feature has been identified.
- ● Where supporting information has been added.

2 Now add a second feature with supporting information.

Feature 2: _____

_____

Question 2: Source analysis

Question 2 is divided into two parts.

- ● Question 2(a) is a utility question on two sources. You have to explain how useful each source is to a historical enquiry.

- ● Question 2(b) is an analysis question that asks you to use sources – you have to explain a follow-up enquiry and the source that you would use.

Question 2(a): Utility

Below is an example of a utility question which is worth 8 marks. The sources will be labelled Source A and Source B.

Study Sources A and B. How useful are Sources A and B for an enquiry into the problems the police faced when investigating the Ripper murders? Explain your answer, using Sources A and B and your own knowledge of the historical context. (8 marks)

SOURCE A

Part of a picture printed on the front page of the Illustrated Police News, *October 1888.*

SOURCE B

From a report on a public demonstration in Bethnal Green, published in the Pall Mall Gazette, *1 October 1888.*

After several speeches upon the conduct of the Home Secretary and Sir Charles Warren, a resolution was unanimously passed that it was high time both officers should resign and make way for some officers who would leave no stone unturned for the purpose of bringing the murderers to justice, instead of allowing them to run riot in a civilised city like London.

How to answer

- Explain the value and limitations of the contents of each source and try to add some contextual knowledge when you make a point.

- Explain the value and limitations of the **provenance** of each source and try to add some contextual knowledge when you make a point.

- In your conclusion give a final judgement on the relative value of each source. For example, one source might provide one view of an event, the other source a different view.

> **Key term**
>
> **Provenance** Who wrote or created the source, when, and for what purpose. This can have a big impact on what the sources tells us.

Below is part of a sample Level 3 answer to this question in which is explained the utility of Source A. Read it and the comments around it.

> Source A is useful because it suggests that newspapers complicated the investigation by printing their own pictures of suspects. These unofficial sketches of 'foreign'-looking suspects increased tensions towards immigrants, especially Jewish people. Sensational stories and pictures also encouraged hoax letters from men claiming to be the Ripper and this wasted police time. The usefulness of Source A is further enhanced by its provenance. It is a front page from the news-sheet 'Illustrated Police News' and was published in October 1888 at the time when the investigation was in full swing. However, a historian must be careful because it may not be typical of the many other newspapers reporting on the investigation at the time.

A judgement is made on the value of the content of the source.

Own knowledge is used to support this judgement.

The provenance of the source is taken into account when making a judgement on its utility.

✎ Analysing provenance

Now write your own Level 3 answer on Source B. Remember to take into account how the provenance affects the usefulness of the source content.

Question 2(b): Framing a historical enquiry

Below is an example of a source question requiring you to frame an enquiry. This is worth 4 marks.

How could you follow up Source B to find out more how the public felt about the Ripper investigation? In your answer, you must give the question you would ask and the type of source you could use.

How to answer

You have to identify a follow-up enquiry and explain how you would carry this out. For each of the questions you are given space to write. Below is a sample answer to this question with comments around it.

Detail in Source B that I would follow up:

I would follow up on what the reporter says about the several speeches that were made.

The follow-up enquiry is identified.

Question I would ask:

What specific criticisms were made of the Home Secretary and Sir Charles Warren in the speeches?

The linked question is asked.

What type of source I could use:

Other newspaper accounts.

An appropriate source is identified.

How this might help answer my question:

Other news reports might give more detailed accounts about the actual content of the speeches and the arguments used to attack both men.

An explanation of how the source would help with the follow-up enquiry.

Question 3: Similarity or difference

Below is an example of a similarity or difference question which is worth 4 marks.

Explain one way in which trials were similar in the middle ages and seventeenth centuries.

How to answer

- Explain the similarity or difference between the two time periods.
- Use specific information from both time periods to support the comparison, showing good knowledge and understanding.

Below is a sample answer to this with comments around it.

During the middle ages trial by cold water was sometimes used to decide guilt or innocence. The accused was tied with a knot above their waist and lowered into the water on the end of a rope. During the seventeenth century, the similar 'swimming' test was used in cases of witchcraft. People believed that the innocent would sink and the guilty would float. If they floated, the accused would be examined for the 'Devil's marks' as a final proof of witchcraft.

The method of trial by cold water used in the middle ages is identified.

Own knowledge is used to support this.

The similar use of the swim test in the seventeenth century is identified.

Own knowledge is used to support this.

Develop the detail

Below is a question and part of an answer. Read the answer and add the missing detail.

Explain one way in which policing methods were different in the later middle ages and the nineteenth century.

> In the later middle ages policing was the responsibility of the local community. However, in the nineteenth century the first professional police force was established.

Question 4: Causation

Below is an example of a causation question which is worth 12 marks.

Explain why there were changes to policing in the period between c.1700 and c.1900.

You may use the following in your answer.
- Individuals
- Increased taxation

You **must** also include information of your own.

How to answer

- You need to explain at least three causes. This could be the two mentioned in the question and one of your own. You don't have to use the points given in the question, you could decide to make more points of your own instead.
- You need to fully explain each cause and support your explanation with precise knowledge, ensuring that each cause is fully focused on in the question.

Below is part of an answer to the question:

> There were huge changes to policing in the first half on the nineteenth century. Firstly, Robert Peel played an important individual role in introducing the Metropolitan Police Force in London in 1829. Secondly, the government was more involved in people's lives and had more money which could be used to set up the first police force.
>
> For hundreds of years policing had been just the responsibility of local people. In 1829, 3200 professional and full-time police officers started to patrol the streets of London and this paved the way for further police forces across the country.

Changes to policing are mentioned. However, there is no explicit focus on the question.

The supporting evidence is not precise enough and lacks detail.

The answer is losing focus on the question.

 Make an improvement

Try improving the answer. An example of a better answer to this question is on page 53 for you to check your own answer against.

Answers and quick quizzes at **www.hoddereducation.co.uk/myrevisionnotes**

Your point is a short answer to the question. You then back this up with lots of examples to demonstrate all the knowledge you have learned during your studies: this is the section that proves you have studied and revised, rather than just guessing. Finally, you will link that knowledge to the question by explaining in a final sentence.

- Point: passing my GCSE History exam will be very helpful in the future.
- Example: for example, it will help me to continue my studies next year.
- Explain: this will help me to get the job I want in the future.

Below is a sample answer to the causation question on page 52 with comments around it.

> **Exam tip**
>
> Writing a good paragraph to explain an answer to something is as easy as PEEing – Point, Example, Explain.

The first ever police force in Britain was set up in London in 1829. One cause for this huge development was the role of Sir Robert Peel, the Home Secretary at the time. Peel had to convince his fellow politicians who feared a police force might be used to limit people's freedom. He reassured them that this was not the case and used statistics to demonstrate how crime was increasing. This further strengthened the arguments for supporting the Metropolitan Police Act.

> The first cause is introduced and immediately focuses on the question.

> The supporting evidence is precise and relevant to the question.

Another reason politicians supported the introduction of a police force was because it was no longer seen as too expensive. The government had become more involved in people's lives and the war with France had forced it to raise more money by increasing taxes. Local authorities were given powers to raise taxes and this increased revenue meant that the costs of a police force could now be met.

> The second cause is introduced and immediately focuses on the question.

> The supporting evidence is precise and relevant to the question.

The government also feared the possibility of revolution and this was another reason to support a police force. High food prices and growing unemployment had led to more protests, demonstrations and even riots after 1815. The government viewed revolution as a real threat and therefore Peel and others could argue that a police force was needed to stop such demonstrations getting out of hand.

> The third cause is introduced and immediately focuses on the question. Notice that this is a cause not mentioned in the question.

> The supporting evidence is precise and relevant to the question.

 Now have a go

Explain why the authorities took vagabondage so seriously in the period c.1500–c.1700.

> You may use the following in your answer:
> - Attitudes in society
> - Printed pamphlets
>
> You **must** also use information of your own.

Questions 5 and 6: A judgement about change, continuity and significance

Below is an example of questions 5 and 6 which asks you to make a judgement about how far you agree with the statement. It is worth 20 marks (4 of these are for spelling, punctuation, grammar and the use of specialist terminology).

'The activities of Matthew Hopkins were the main reason why witchcraft accusations increased in the seventeenth century.' Do you agree? Explain your answer.

> You may use the following in your answer.
> - Attitudes in society
> - Religious uncertainty
>
> You **must** also include information of your own.

How to answer

You need to give a balanced answer which agrees and disagrees with the statement using evidence from the bullet points as well as your own knowledge. Here is one way you could approach this:

- agree with the view with evidence from a bullet point and your own knowledge
- disagree with the view with evidence, possibly from the other bullet point and your own knowledge
- agree/disagree with the view (depending on the statement) with another point from your own knowledge
- make a final judgement on whether you agree or disagree with the statement.

Below is part of an answer to this question which agrees with the view given in the statement.

The increased number of witchcraft accusations during the seventeenth century was partly the result of the activities of Matthew Hopkins. Between 1645 and 1647 Hopkins and his assistant searched East Anglia for witches and collected evidence against 36 people, most elderly women. Hopkins got confessions by keeping suspects standing, on the move and awake for days. He identified any scar, boil or spot found on a suspect as a 'Devil's mark' from which familiars sucked the witch's blood. These confessions reinforced attitudes in society and people's fears of witchcraft. Towns and villages across East Anglia summoned Hopkins to rid them of their witches.

> The answer immediately focuses on the question.

> Support is provided from own knowledge.

> Explanation is provided using the first bullet point.

 Now have a go

1 Have a go at another paragraph by disagreeing with the view given in the statement and using the second bullet point.
2 Write another paragraph that disagrees or agrees with the statement using another point from your own knowledge.
3 Write a conclusion giving your final judgement on the question.

Answers and quick quizzes at **www.hoddereducation.co.uk/myrevisionnotes**